APICIUS
DE RE COQUINARIA

This book has been translated and completed by cross analysing ancient latin editions. First published in 2021 by a passionate latinist and chef.
You have the right to distribute, remix, adapt, and build upon the material in any medium or format as long as attribution is given to this book.

CONTENT

BOOK I
page 9

BOOK II
page 23

MINCED MEATS & SAUSAGES..25
HYDROGARUM, ROUX, APOTHERMUM..................................28
SOW WOMB & BLOOD SAUSAGE..31
LUCANIAN SAUSAGE... 32
OTHER SAUSAGES...33

BOOK III
page 35

TURNING VEGETABLES A BEAUTIFUL GREEN.......................37
FOOD FOR THE STOMACH..38
ASPARAGUS...40
GOURDS...41
PUMPKIN... 43
CUCUMBERS...44
WATERMELON & MELON.. 45
MALLOW...46
CABBAGE SPROUTS & STALKS..47
LEEKS...49
BEETS...50
ALEXANDERS...51
TURNIPS OR NAVEWS...52
HORSERADISH...53
MASHED GREENS..54
FIELD HERBS..55
NETTLES..56
CHICORY & LETTUCE...57
CARDOONS...59
ARTICHOKE HEARTS..60
CARROTS OR PARSNIPS...62

BOOK IV
page 63

JELLIED DISHES..65
FISH, VEGETABLE AND FRUIT DISHES..................................67
MINUTALS (MINCED DISHES)..80
GRUELS..83
STEWS..84

BOOK V
page 87

PORRIDGES...89
LENTILS...90
PEAS...92
PEAS & BEANS IN THE POD...96
BARLEY AND SPELT GRUELS.. 99
GREEN PODS & STALKS & BAIAE BEANS............................. 100
FENUGREEK.. 101
BEANS & CHICKPEAS..102

BOOK VI
page 103

OSTRICH..105
CRANES & DUCKS..106
PATRIDGE, GROUSE & TURTLEDOVE......................................109
PIGEONS & FATTENED DOVES..110
DIFFERENT BIRDS, THRUSHES, PEAFOWL, PHEASANT, GOOSE.. 111
STRONG SMELLING BIRDS..113
FLAMINGOS & PARROTS... 114
GOOSE...116
CHICKEN 117

BOOK VII
page 123

STERILE SOW WOMBS, RIND, TENDERLOIN, TAIL & FEET............125
SOW'S UDDER..127
FIG-FED SOW'S LIVER.. 128
TID-BITS... 129

ROASTS	131
BOILED MEATS & PORK SLICES	133
STOMACH	136
KIDNEYS	137
HAM	138
LIVERS & LUNGS	140
HOME SWEET CAKES WITH HONEY	141
BULBS	144
FARN MUSHROOMS & CAESAR MUSHROOMS	145
TRUFFLES	147
TARO	149
SNAILS	150
EGGS	151

BOOK VIII
page 153

WILD BOAR	155
DEER	158
ROEDEER	160
WILD SHEEP	161
BEEF OR VEAL	162
KID OR LAMB	163
SUCKLING PIG	167
HARE	173
DORMOUSE	178

BOOK IX
page 179

SPINY LOBSTER & CRAB	181
ELECTRIC RAY	183
CALAMARI	184
CUTTLEFISH	185
OCTOPUS	186
OYSTER	187
SHELLFISH	188
SEA URCHIN	189
MUSSELS	191
BONITO & YOUNG TUNA	192
SEA MULLET	194
CATFISH, YOUNG TUNA & TUNA	195

RED MULLET..196
BAIAN STEW..197

BOOK X
page 199

DIFFERENTS KINDS OF FISH...201
CONGER..203
HORNED FISH...204
MULLET..205
YOUNG TUNA... 206
PERCH... 207
RED SEABREAM...208
MURENA...209
SCOMBER & MACKEREL..211
TUNA.. 212
DENTEX..213
GILT HEAD BREAM 214
SCORPIONFISH... 215
EEL..216

APICIUS

BOOK I
EPIMELES (THE DILIGENT)

WONDERFUL SPICED WINE
(CONDITUM PARADOXUM).

Pour into a brass vase 2 sextarii *(38.5 ounces / 1086ml)* of wine and 15 parts of honey.
Heat on a slow wood fire, constantly stirring the mixture with a spatula.
When the liquid starts boiling, add some dashes of wine drop by drop unless you prefer to stop the boiling by taking the mixture out of the fire.
When the mixture has cooled down, make it boil again.
Repeat this a second time, and then a third.
Remove from the fire and let it rest till the next day.
The next day, skim the mixture.
Add 4 ounces *(110g)* of pepper, 3 scruples *(0.12oz / 3.42g)* of grounded mastic, 1 drachm *(3g)* of nard, 1 drachm *(3g)* of saffron, 5 dried dates that have been pitted and crushed after macerating in wine.
Once done, pour 18 sextarii *(346oz / 9774ml)* of sweet wine.
Boil the mixture.

SPICED HONEY WINE
(CONDITUM MELIZOMUM).

This unalterable honey wine is given to wayfarers.

In a small barrel pour skimmed honey mixed with ground pepper.
At the moment of drinking, mix the honey with the wine.
It is recommended to pour some wine into the honey mixture *(melizomum)* to facilitate it's flow.

ROMAN WORMWOOD WINE
(ABSINTHIATUM ROMANUM).

Take one Theban ounce *(from the city of Thebes. Unknown value)* of Roman wormwood *(Artemisia Pontica)* from the Pontus *(Region on the southern coast of the Black Sea)*.
Take one Theban ounce of mastic, 3 scruples *(0.12oz / 3.42g)* of nard leaves, 6 scruples *(0.24oz / 6.84g)* of costus *(Saussurea costus)*, 3 scruples *(0.12oz / 3.42g)* of saffron and 18 sextarii of old wine.
The bitterness of this mix requires that we stick to maceration and not cooking it.

ROSE WINE
(ROSATUM).

Remove the white part on the extremity of rose petals.
String the petals in a rosary.
Leave as many petals as you can to macerate for 7 days in wine. Then remove them.
In the same manner, string new fresh petals in a necklace and leave them to macerate 7 days in the wine. Then remove them.
Repeat a third time and filter the wine.
Before drinking, add some honey.
Choose only the best quality roses and free from dew.

VIOLET WINE
(VIOLATUM).

Made in the same way as the rose wine but with fresh violets. Also add honey.

ROSE WINE WITHOUT ROSES
(ROSATUM SINE ROSA).

Fill a small palm leaf basket with lemon tree green leaves.
Immerse the basket in a barrel of must not yet fermented and leave it 40 days.
Remove the basket of leaves.
Add honey before drinking, and use it as rose wine.

LIBURNIAN OIL
(OLEUM LIBURNICUM).

In Spanish *(olive)* oil add elecampane, nutgrass and green laurel leaves, all of it grounded, passed through a sieve and reduced to a very fine powder.
Then add roasted ground salt.
Stir with care during 3 days or more.
Then allow to settle for some time.
Everybody will think it's Liburnian *(region along the Adriatic coast—in modern Croatia)* oil.

WHITE WINE FROM BLACK WINE
(VINUM EX ATRO CANDIDUM).

In a bottle of black wine put bean starch or three egg whites.
Stir for a long time. The next day the wine will be white.
The same result can be obtained with the ashes of white grape vine branches.

OF IMPROVING GARUM
(DE LIQUAMINE EMENDANDO)

If the garum smells bad, fumigate a container over a laurel and cypress fire, and pour the garum inside, after ventilating it.

If it's too salty, add a part of honey that's equal to $\frac{1}{6}^{th}$ of it's volume, stir and the garum is improved.
New must produces the same effect.

OF PRESERVING MEAT WITHOUT SALT AT ANY TIME
(UT CARNES SINE SALE QUOVIS
TEMPORE SINT RECENTES)

Cover the fresh meat with honey and hang it in it's vessel. Use as needed; it will work better in winter, in summer the meat will only last a few days.
Cooked meat is treated likewise.

OF PRESERVING RINDS,
PORK TENDERLOIN AND BOILED FEET
(CALLUM PORCINUM VEL LUMBULUM,
ET UNGELLÆ COCTÆ, UT DIU DURENT)

Preserve them in mustard, prepared with vinegar, salt and honey.
You'll be pleasantly surprised when comes the time to eat it.

OF DESALTING MEAT
(UT CARNEM SALSAM DULCEM FACIAS)

Cook the salty meat in milk, and then in water.

OF PRESERVING FRIED FISH
(UT PISCES FRICTI DIU DURENT)

Immediately after they are fried pour hot vinegar over them.

OF PRESERVING OYSTERS
(OSTREA UT DIU DURENT)

Coat a vinegar container or any other with pitch, wash it with vinegar and lay the oysters in it.

OF MAKING SILPHIUM GO A LONG WAY
(UT UNCIA LASERIS TOTO TEMPORE UTARIS)

Put an ounce of silphium in a spacious jar with about 20 pine nuts. When you'll need silphium, grind the nuts and mix the powder with your food and sauces. Replace the nuts taken with the same number of fresh ones.

OF MAKING HONEY CAKES LAST
(UT DULCIA DE MELLE DIU DURENT)

When it is time to make a cake, take what the Greeks call πηνίον *(yeast)* and mix it with the flour and the honey.

OF IMPROVING A SPOILED HONEY
(UT MEL MALUM BONUM FACIES)

You can turn honey into a saleable product by mixing one part of spoiled honey with two parts of good honey.

OF IDENTIFYING A SPOILED HONEY
(MEL CORRUPTUM UT PROBES)

Immerse a branch of elecampane in honey and light it.
If the honey ignites, it is not spoiled.

OF PRESERVING GRAPES
(UVÆ UT DIU SERVENTUR)

Take perfect grapes from the vines.
Boil rain water down to one third of its volume.
Pour it in a vessel with the raisins
The vessel must be pitched and sealed with plaster, and be kept in a cool place to which the sun has no access.
Treated in this manner, the grapes will be fresh whenever you need them.

This water can be given as mead to the sick.
You can also preserve the grapes by covering them with barley, they will be kept intact.

OF PRESERVING APPLES AND POMEGRANATES
(UT MALA GRANATA DIU DURENT)

Steep them into boiling water, take them out immediately and hang them up.

OF KEEPING QUINCES
(UT MALA CYDONIA DIU SERVENTUR)

Pick out perfect quinces with stems and leaves.
Place them in a vessel, cover them with honey and boiled down grape must to half of the original volume *(defrutum)* They'll stay preserved for a long time.

OF PRESERVING FRESH FIGS, APPLES, PLUMS, PEARS AND CHERRIES
(FICUM RECENTEM, MALA, PRUNA, PIRA, CERASIA UT DIU SERVES)

Pick these fruits carefully with the stems on and place them in honey without letting them touch each other.

OF PRESERVING CITRUS
(CITRIA UT DIU DURENT)

Place each citrus in a glass vessel, one per vessel, which is then sealed with plaster and suspended.

OF PRESERVING MULBERRIES
(MORA UT DIU DURENT)

Press mulberries to extract the juice and cook it.
Mix it with sapa *(cooked wine must reduced to ⅓rd)*.

Pour in a glass vessel and place the *(intact)* mulberries inside.
They fruits will stay preserved for a long time.

OF PRESERVING VEGETABLES
(OLERA UT DIU SERVENTUR)

Pick vegetables before they're completely mature in a pitched vessel.

OF KEEPING KOHLRABI
(RAPA UT DIU SERVENTUR)

Clean them.
Place them in a vessel and cover them with myrtle berries, honey and vinegar.
Alternative way: mix mustard with honey, vinegar and salt, place the kohlrabi in a vessel and cover with the mixture.

OF PRESERVING TRUFFLES
(TUBERA UT DIU SERVENTUR)

Select truffles that water hasn't damaged.
Place them in a vase separating them with very dry sawdust.
Seal the vessel with plaster and deposit it in a cool place.

OF PRESERVING CLINGSTONE PEACHES
(DURACINA PERFICA UT DIU DURENT)

Select the best peaches and place them in brine *(muria)*.
The next day remove them from the salt water, sponge carefully and place them into a vessel.
Sprinkle salt on the fruits, vinegar and garden savory.

AROMATIC SALT FOR VARIOUS USES
(SALES CONDITI AD MULTA)

These aromatic salts are used to help digestion, bowel movement, against all illness and pestilence, as well as to prevent colds.
They are more pleasant to the taste than you would expect:
1 lb. of common ground salt
2 lb. of roasted ground ammoniac salt *(found under sand, from the greek* ἄμμος*)*
3 oz. of white pepper
2 oz. of ginger
1½ oz. of ammi *(Ajwain)*
1½ oz. of thyme
1½ oz. of celery seed. Or 3 oz. of parsley.
3 oz. of oregano
1½ oz. of rocket seed
3 oz. of black pepper
1 oz. of saffron
2 oz. of hyssop *(Cretan Hyssop)*
2 oz. of nard leaves
2 oz. of parsley
2 oz. of anise

OF PRESERVING GREEN OLIVES
& MAKING OLIVE OIL WHEN WANTED
(OLIVAS VIRIDES SERVARE
& QUOVIS TEMPORE OLEUM FACIES)

Keep in oil the olives picked from the tree.
They'll stay the same as if you just picked them from the tree.
You can make green oil from them when you desire.

CUMIN SAUCE FOR OYSTER AND SHELLFISH
(CUMINATUM IN OSTREA & CONCHYLIA)

Pepper, lovage, parsley, dry mint, leaves of silphium and malabathrum *(Pogostemon Patchouli)*, plenty of cumin, honey, vinegar and garum.
Alternative way: pepper, lovage, parsley, dry mint, plenty of cumin, honey, vinegar, garum.

SILPHIUM SAUCE
(LASERATUM)

Dissolve Cyrenaic or Parthian silphium in lukewarm water, add garum mixed with vinegar.
Or: grind and dissolve pepper, parsley, dry mint, silphium root, honey, vinegar, garum.
Alternative: pepper, caraway, dill, parsley, dry mint, silphium leaves, turnsole, malabathrum *(Pogostemon Patchouli)*, Indian nard, a little costus *(Saussurea costus)*, honey, vinegar, garum.

WINE SAUCE FOR TRUFFLES
(OENOGARUM AD TUBERA)

Pepper, lovage, coriander, rue *(ruta graveolens)*, garum *(made with wine)*, honey and little oil.
Alternative: thyme, savory, pepper, lovage, honey, garum *(made with wine)* and oil.

VINEGAR SAUCE
(OXYPORON)

Oxyporon was used to improve or activate digestion.

2 oz. of cumin
1 oz. of ginger
1 oz. of green rue
6 scruples *(0.24oz. / 6.84g)* of salt peter

12 scruples *(0.48oz. / 13.68g)* of plump dates,
1 oz. of pepper
9 oz. of honey.
Macerate in vinegar the Ethiopian, Syrian or Libyan cumin. Drain and grind the cumin with the other ingredients. Thicken by adding the honey, and add some vinegar garum if necessary.

SAUCE MADE OF ALL SORTS OF CONDIMENTS (HYPOTRIMMA)

Like Oxyporon, Hypotrimma was used to activate digestion.

Pepper, lovage, dry mint, pine nuts, dried raisins *(under the sun)*, date *(caryote)*, fresh unsalted cheese, honey, vinegar, garum, oil, boiled down grape must to half of the original volume (*defrutum*) or date wine *(caryotum)*.

VINEGAR DIGESTIVE GARUM (OXYGARUM)

½ oz. of pepper
3 scruples *(0.12oz / 3.42g)* of gallic seseli *(seseli tortuosum)*
6 scruples *(0.24oz. / 6.84g)* of cardamom
6 scruples *(0.24oz. / 6.84g)* of cumin
1 scruple *(0.04oz. / 1.14g)* of leaves,
6 scruples *(0.24oz. / 6.84g)* of dried mint.
Grind, pass through a sieve and bound with honey.
When you want to use it, add some garum and vinegar.
Alternative: 1 oz. each of pepper, parsley, carraway and lovage, grind and mix with honey.
When you want to use it, add some garum and vinegar.

MORTARIA (MORETARIA)

Moretaria preparations are made in a mortar.

Mint, rue *(ruta graveolens)*, coriander and fennel (all fresh), lovage, pepper, honey, garum.
Add some vinegar before use.

APICIUS

BOOK II
SARCOPTES (THE BUTCHER)

MINCED MEATS & SAUSAGES

HYDROGARUM, ROUX, APOTHERMUM

SOW WOMB & BLOOD SAUSAGE

LUCANIAN SAUSAGE

OTHER SAUSAGES

I.
MINCED MEATS & SAUSAGES

MINCED SEAFOOD
(ISICIA)

Mince shrimps, lobsters, squids, cuttlefishes, crayfishes.
Season the preparation with pepper, cumin and silphium root.

CUTTLEFISH SAUSAGE
(ISICIA DE LOLIGINE)

Get rid of the cuttlefish's tail.
Chop the cuttlefish finely and pound in mortar until mush.
Knead with some garum.
Shape the mixture into sausages.

MANTIS SQUILLIS SAUSAGE
(ISICIA DE SQUILLIS)

Peel the mantis shrimps or big shrimps to extract the meat.
Pound the meat in the mortar with pepper and highest quality garum.
Shape the mixture into sausages.

CREPINETTES
(OMENTATA)

Roast a pork liver and remove the veins.
Grind pepper and rue *(ruta graveolens)* into garum.
Add the liver, pound and mix.
Shape into small sausages, wrap them in a laurel leaf.

Put them to smoke where you can leave them as long as you want.

When you'll want to eat them, take them out of the smoke, and roast.

BRAIN SAUSAGE
(ISICIA DE CEREBELLIS)

Place in a mortar pepper, lovage and oregano.
Grind and moisten with garum.
Add cooked *(pork)* brains and mix until no lumps are left.
Incorporate 5 eggs and keep mixing until you have a smooth mush.
Thin with garum.
Pour in a brass pan and cook.
When cooked lay on a cutting board. Dice.
Place in a mortar pepper, lovage and oregano, grind and mix, boil in an earthen pot *(with honey, vinegar and garum)*,
When boilt shred dried bread in the pot to thicken.
Pour this sauce in a mushroom dish *(on the diced meat)*.
Sprinkle with pepper and serve.

SPONDYLUS SAUSAGE
(ISICIA DE SPONDYLIS)

Boil the spondylus *(spondylus gaederopus)*
Pound the meat.
Mix this with boilt spelt and eggs.
Season with pepper.
Wrap in caul *(after shaping into sausages)* and grill.
Pour wine garum over them and serve like isicia

CREPINETTE SAUSAGE
(ISICIA OMENTATA)

Mix minced pork meat with the soft part of wine macerated oatmeal bread.

Pound with pepper and garum, if you like add some seeded myrtle berries.

Shape into small rolls, add pine nuts and peppercorns.

Wrap them in caul and braise.

Serve with boiled down grape must to two-thirds of the original volume *(carœnum)*.

II.
HYDROGARUM, ROUX, APOTHERMUM

FULL SAUSAGES
(ISICIA PLENA)

Take fresh pheasant fat, brown and cut into dices.
Season with pepper, garum and boiled down grape must to two-thirds of the original volume *(carænum)*.
Stuff small casings with the preparation.
Cook the sausages in hydrogarum *(7:1 part water:garum)*

MINCED MEAT IN HYDROGARUM
(HYDROGARATA ISICIA)

Crush pepper, lovage and just a little bit of pellitory *(perythrum)*.
Spread over the garum and well water in desired quantity.
Mix and pour over the minced meat in a pan.
Cook slowly and serve without reducing the sauce.

SAUCE FOR CHICKEN SAUSAGES
(IN ISICIA DE PULLO)

This recipe might be incomplete

1 lb. of virgin oil *(olive)*
¼ lb. of garum
½ oz. of pepper

SAUCE FOR CHICKEN SAUSAGES II
(ALITER DE PULLO)

Grind 31 peppercorns.

Add a cup *(calicem)* of high quality garum, and of the same amount of boiled down grape must to two-thirds of the original volume *(caraenum)*.
6 cups *(calicem)* of water.
Add honey and cook over the smoke of a fire.

SIMPLE SAUSAGE
(ISICIUM SIMPLEX)

For 1 acetabulum *(2.30 fl oz / 68mL)* of garum, add 7 of water.
Some green celery *(apius viridis)*.
A spoonful *(cochlear = ¼ cyathus = 0.38 fl oz / 11.25mL)* of ground pepper.
Boil the sausage in it.
If you intend taking this to relax the belly, add potassium tartrate *(faeces conditi from aromatic wine lees)* to your hydrogarum.

OF THE BEST SAUSAGES
(ISICIA)

Peacock sausages are the best of all if they are fried and if the meat lost it's toughness. Then comes pheasant sausages, third comes the rabbit ones, the chicken ones fourth and the young suckling pig fifth.

ROUX FOR SAUSAGES
(ISICIA AMYLATA SIC FACIES)

Ground pepper, lovage, oregano, some silphium, a pinch of ginger and a little bit of honey.
Add garum and mix.
Pour on the sausages and put to boil.
When boilt, thicken with starch, and serve.

ROUX FOR SAUSAGES II
(ALITER ISICIA AMYLATA SIC FACIES)

Grind pepper which has been macerated overnight.
Pour garum over the pepper little by little until you get a thick well grinded pepper sauce.

ROUX FOR SAUSAGES III
(ALITER ISICIA AMYLATA SIC FACIES)

Bone a chicken and cook *(the bones)* in an earthen pot with leeks, dill and salt.
When the broth is done, place in a mortar pepper, celery seed and soaked rice.
Grind everything, add garum and raisin wine *(passum)* or boiled down grape must to half of the original volume *(defrutum)*.
Mix this sauce *(with the broth)*.
Serve with the *(chicken)* croquettes.

APOTHERMUM
(APOTHERMUM)

Take boilt spelt, peeled pine nuts and peeled almonds, that have macerated in water and blanched with clay *(creta argentaria)*, so they keep their whiteness.
Mix these ingredients, add raisins, boiled down grape must to two-thirds of the original volume *(carænum)* or raisin wine.
Serve in a mushroom dish and sprinkle with breadcrumbs.

III.
SOW WOMB & BLOOD SAUSAGE

STUFFED SOW WOMB
(VULVULÆ BOTELLI)

Ground pepper and cumin, two small heads of leeks peeled until white, rue *(ruta graveolens)* and garum are mixed with the *(pork)* meat finely minced.
Pound this preparation until smooth, then add peppercorns and pine nuts.
Stuff the mix in well cleaned sow womb, that you'll cook with water, oil, garum and a bunch of leeks and dill.

BLOOD SAUSAGE
(BOTELLUM)

To 6 cooked egg yolks and chopped pine nuts, mix onion, minced leek, ground pepper, moon carrot *(tus—libanotis)* and fresh blood.
Stuff in casings and cook in wine and garum.

IV.
LUCANIAN SAUSAGE

LUCANIAN SAUSAGE
(LUCANICÆ)

Proceed like above. Ground pepper, cumin, savory, rue *(ruta graveolens)*, parsley, seasoning *(condimentum)* and laurel berries with garum.

Mix with finely minced pork and keep pounding, after adding more garum.

Blend whole pepper, lard in abundance and pine nuts into the mixture.

Stuff in small intestine casings and hang the sausages to smoke.

V.
OTHER SAUSAGES

FARCIMINA
(FARCIMINA)

Pound eggs and pork brains, pine nuts, pepper, garum and a little silphium.
Stuff casings with the mixture.
Parboil the farcimina then roast them and serve.

FARCIMINA II
(ALITER FARCIMINA)

Mix cooked and pounded spelt with chopped pork.
Pound the mixture with pepper, garum and pine nuts.
Fill the casings, parboil and fry with salt.
Serve with mustard, or on a round dish, in slices.

FARCIMINA III
(ALITER FARCIMINA)

Wash spelt and boil it with intestine garum and finely cut leeks.
Take the mixture out of the fire, finely chop lard and fresh pork, and mix everything.
Crush pepper, lovage and 3 eggs.
Mix all in a mortar with pine nuts and whole pepper.
Add garum. Stuff the casings, parboil and then grill them at low temperature, or serve boiled.

ROUND SAUSAGE
(CIRCELLOS ISICIATOS)

Stuff casings with minced meat and give them a round shape.

Smoke the sausages. When their color gets red from the smoke, grill them lightly.

Place them with care on a dish and pour over a thick wine garum, with cumin inside.

APICIUS

BOOK III

CEPUROS (THE GARDENER)

TURNING VEGETABLES A BEAUTIFUL GREEN
FOOD FOR THE STOMACH
ASPARAGUS
GOURDS
PUMPKIN
CUCUMBERS
WATERMELON & MELON
MALLOW
CABBAGE SPROUTS & STALKS
LEEKS
BEETS
ALEXANDERS
TURNIPS OR NAVEWS
HORSERADISH
MASHED GREENS
FIELD HERBS
NETTLES
CHICORY & LETTUCE
CARDOONS
CARROTS OR PARSNIPS

I.
TURNING VEGETABLES A BEAUTIFUL GREEN

TURNING VEGETABLES A BEAUTIFUL GREEN
(DE OLERIBUS UT OMNE OLUS SMARAGDINUM FIAT)

To obtain vegetables of a beautiful green cook them in saltpeter.

II.
FOOD FOR THE STOMACH

FOOD FOR THE STOMACH
(PULMENTARIUM AD VENTREM)

Parboil minced beets and aged *(matured more after picking)* leeks.
Place them on a baking dish.
Grind pepper, cumin, add broth and raisin wine, to add sweetness to the sauce.
Boil and serve.

FOOD FOR THE STOMACH II
(SIMILITER PULMENTARIUM AD VENTREM)

Soak polypody in lukewarm water to soften it.
Grate it, and crush pepper and cumin.
Sprinkle this spice mix on boiling vegetables and serve.

FOOD FOR THE STOMACH III
(ALITER AD VENTREM)

Grate beets without washing them.
In the middle place some saltpeter.
Cook in water. During cooking add raisin wine or boiled down grape must to two-thirds of the original volume *(carœnum)*, cumin, sprinkle with pepper and a little bit of oil.
Bring to a boil. Crush polypody and nuts with garum.
Pour in your boiling pot, cover, take off the fire quickly and serve.

BEETS THE VARRO WAY
(BETACEOS VARRONIS)

This recipe is also a laxative.

Take black beets, clean them and cook them in honeyed wine *(mulsum)* with a little bit of salt and oil, or with salt, water and oil, and boiling it down.
Prepare this way the broth and drink it. It will be better if you cook a chicken in it.

ANOTHER LAXATIVE
(ALITER AD VENTREM)

Take green celery *(apius veridis)* with its roots, clean it and dry it in the sun.
Make it boil in a new earthen pot with some leek bottom and top. Boil down to a third of it's volume.
Thereupon grind pepper and garum in a mortar, add honey and mix.
Strain and pour the broth in the mortar. Boil again, the celery in the soup and serve. If desired, serve the celery with the soup.

III.
ASPARAGUS

ASPARAGUS
(ASPARAGOS)

Dry some asparagus. Immerse them in hot water where you will cook them very little so they can stay crisp.

IV.
GOURDS

GOURD
(CUCURBITAS)

Arrange on a dish cooked and drained gourds.
Place in a mortar pepper, cumin, a little silphium root, a little rue *(ruta graveolens)*, moisten with some garum and vinegar, and pour boiled down grape must to half of the original volume *(defrutum)* on these ingredients to colour the sauce.
Pour the sauce on your dish.
Let it boil three times, take off the fire and sprinkle with just a little bit of pepper.

TARO STYLE GOURDS
(CUCURBITAS IURE COLOCASIORUM)

Boil the gourds in water like preparing taro.
Grind pepper, cumin and rue.
Moisten with vinegar and garum, and mix.
Pour this sauce in an earthen pot.
Put the drained gourd pieces in.
Put to a boil, bind with starch, sprinkle with pepper and serve.

ALEXANDRIA STYLE GOURDS
(CUCURBITAS MORE ALEXANDRINO)

Boil the gourds, drain them, salt them, and place in a baking dish.
Grind pepper, cumin, coriander seed, green mint and silphium root.

Moisten with vinegar, add dates *(caryote)*, and pine nuts, then grind.
Add honey, vinegar, garum, boiled down grape must to half of the original volume *(defrutum)* and oil.
Pour the mix over the gourds. When cooked, sprinkle with pepper and serve.

BOILED GOURD
(CUCURBITAS ELIXATAS)

Stewed in garum, oil and wine.

FRIED GOURD
(CUCURBITAS FRICTAS)

Fried with basic wine garum and pepper.

BOILED & FRIED GOURD
(CUCURBITAS ELIXATAS & FRICTAS)

Place them on a baking dish.
Pour a cumin sauce over, with a little oil, put to boil and serve.

FRIED GOURD II
(CUCURBITAS FRICTAS TRITAS)

Grind pepper, lovage, cumin, oregano and onion in a blend of wine, garum and oil.
Bind with starch and pour the sauce on the gourds, then serve.

CHICKEN GOURD
(CUCURBITAS CUM GALLINA)

Clingstone peaches, truffles, pepper, caraway, cumin, silphium, green herbs: mint, celery, coriander, pennyroyal, calamint; honey, wine, garum, oil and vinegar.

V.
PUMPKIN

PUMPKIN
(CITRINI)

Hartwort, silphium, dried mint, vinegar, garum.

VI.
CUCUMBER

CUCUMBER
(CUCUMERES)

Peel them and prepare them with garum or wine garum.. They won't cause you flatulence and you'll find them tender.

CUCUMBER II
(ALITER CUCUMERES)

Peel the cucumbers and boil them with pork brains, cumin and a little honey.
During cooking, add celery seed, garum and oil.
Bind with eggs, sprinkle with pepper and serve.

CUCUMBER III
(ALITER CUCUMERES)

Pepper, pennyroyal, honey or raisin wine *(passum)*, garum and vinegar. Silphium can be added sometimes.

VII.
WATERMELON & MELONS

WATERMELON & MELONS
(ALITER CUCUMERES)

Pepper, pennyroyal, honey or raisin wine *(passum)*, garum and vinegar. Silphium can be added sometimes.

VIII.
MALLOWS

MALLOWS
(MALVÆ)

Small mallow *(malva rotundifolia)*: wine garum and garum, oil and vinegar.

Large mallow *(malva silvestris)*: wine garum, pepper, garum, boiled down grape must to two-thirds of the original volume *(carœnum)* or raisin wine.

IX.
CABBAGE SPROUTS & STALKS

CABBAGE SPROUTS AND STALKS
(CIMA & COLICULI)

Sprouts: cumin, salt, old wine and oil. Add, if you wish, pepper, lovage, mint, rue *(ruta graveolens)*, coriander.
Shoot leaves: garum, wine, oil.

CABBAGE SPROUTS AND STALKS II
(ALITER CIMA & COLICULI)

Boil cabbage stalks and cut in half. Mix the leaves with coriander, onion, cumin, pepper, raisin wine or boiled down grape must to two-thirds of the original volume *(carœnum)* and a little oil.

CABBAGE SPROUTS AND STALKS III
(ALITER CIMA & COLICULI)

Boil cabbage stalks and place them in a dish.
Season with garum, oil, pure wine, cumin.
(Braise and) sprinkle with pepper, chopped up leek, cumin and green coriander.

CABBAGE SPROUTS AND STALKS IV
(ALITER COLICULI)

Prepare the cabbage sprouts like previously and cook them with boiled leeks.

CABBAGE SPROUTS AND STALKS V
(ALITER COLICULI)

Prepare the cabbage sprouts like previously, add green olives and boil everything together.

CABBAGE SPROUTS AND STALKS VI
(ALITER COLICULI)

Prepare the cabbage sprouts like previously, cover with boiled spelt and pine nuts.
Sprinkle with raisins.

X.
LEEKS

MATURED LEAKS
(PORROS MATUROS)

A pinch of salt in a mix of water and oil. Cook the leeks in the mixture and then drain them. Serve them with oil, garum and wine.

LEAKS II
(ALITER PORROS)

Cover leeks with leaves and stalks and cook them over hot embers.
Serve like previously.

LEAKS III
(ALITER PORROS)

Cook the leeks in water.
Serve like previously.

LEAKS IV
(ALITER PORROS)

After having boiled the leeks in water, add unseasoned beans in the sauce in which you wish to eat them.

XI.
BEETS

BEETS
(BETÆ)

Chop beets, leeks, coriander and cumin, add some raisins *(uva variana)*, boil all down carefully: bind and serve with garum, oil and vinegar.

BEETS II
(ALITER BETÆ)

Boil the beets and serve them with mustard, a little oil and vinegar.

XII.
ALEXANDERS

ALEXANDERS
(OLISATRA)

Tie in bundles and serve them with garum, oil, and wine, or with grilled fish.

XIII.
TURNIPS OR NAVEWS

TURNIPS OR NAVEWS
(RAPAS SIVE NAPOS)

Boil turnips or navews and drain them. Grind a good amount of cumin and some rue, garum and boiled down grape must to half of the original volume *(defrutum)*, a little silphium, or in the absence, vinegar. Heat and serve.

TURNIPS OR NAVEWS II
(ALITER RAPAS SIVE NAPOS)

Boil turnips or navews, pour oil drop by drop and, if desired, add vinegar.

XIV.
HORSERADISH

HORSERADISHES
(RAPHANI)

Serve with a pepper sauce made by crushing pepper in garum..

XV.
MASHED GREENS

MASHED GREENS
(OLUS MOLLE)

Cook the greens in saltpeter water.
Drain and chop them finely.
Crush pepper, lovage, dried savory and dry onion with garum, oil and wine.

MASHED CELERY
(ALITER OLUS MOLLE)

Cook celery in saltpeter water, drain and chop finely.
Crush in a mortar pepper, lovage, oregano and onion, with wine, garum and oil.
Cook in a pot *(pultario)* and mix in the celery.

MASHED LETTUCE
(ALITER OLUS MOLLE)

Cook lettuce leaves in saltpeter water, drain them and chop finely.
In a mortar crush pepper, lovage, celery seed, dried mint and onion with garum, oil and wine.

OF PRESERVING MASHED GREENS
(OLUS MOLLE NE ACESCAT)

Cut off the bad parts and soak the stems in water to get rid of impurities.
Cover with wormwood.

XVI.
FIELD HERBS

FIELD HERBS
(HERBÆ RUSTICÆ)

With garum, oil and vinegar if eaten raw. Cooked, season them with pepper, cumin and ground mastic berries *(Pistacia lentiscus)*.

XVII.
NETTLES

NETTLE
(URTICÆ)

The female nettle *(Urtica Dioica)*, fights ailments of many kinds when the sun is in the position of the Aries *(March 20 to April 21)*.

XVIII.
CHICORY & LETTUCE

CHICORY
(INTUBA)

In spring dress wild chicory *(Cicorium intybus)* with garum, a little oil and chopped onion.
In winter dress with sour sauce *(embamma)* or with honey and strong vinegar.

LETTUCE
(LACTUCÆ)

Dress the lettuce with oxyporon *(recipe p.14 or just below)*, vinegar and a little bit of garum. It'll help digestion and reduce flatulence.

LETTUCE OXYPORON
(NE LACTUCÆ LÆDANT)

Take as a digestive after eating lettuce

2 oz. of cumin
1 oz. of ginger
1 oz. of green rue
12 scruples *(0.48oz. / 13.68g)* of plump dates,
1 oz. of pepper
8 oz. of honey.
Macerate in vinegar the Ethiopian, Syrian or Libyan cumin. Dry and grind it.
(Grind and) Bind all the spices, when necessary, with honey.

Take half a spoonful after the meal, after mixing it with garum and a little vinegar.

XIX.
CARDOONS

CARDOONS
(CARDUI)

Dress with garum, oil and chopped *(boiled)* eggs.

CARDOONS II
(ALITER CARDUOS)

Crush green herbs: rue *(ruta graveolens)*, mint, coriander, and fennel.
Add pepper, lovage, honey, garum and oil.

XX.
ARTICHOKE HEARTS

ARTICHOKE HEARTS
(SFONDYLI SIVE FUNGULI)

Cook the artichoke hearts in a ordinary wine garum.

ARTICHOKE HEARTS II
(ALITER SFONDYLI)

Boil artichoke hearts in water and then season them with salt, oil, wine, chopped green coriander and whole pepper.

ARTICHOKE HEARTS III
(ALITER SFONDYLI)

Boil artichoke hearts and dress with a starch sauce prepared in this manner: grind celery seed, rue and pepper with raisin wine, garum and a little oil; bind with starch.
Sprinkle with pepper and serve.

ARTICHOKE HEARTS IV
(ALITER SFONDYLI)

Grind together cumin, rue, garum, a little boiled down grape must to two-thirds of the original volume *(carœnum)*, green coriander and leek.
Serve them as pickles.

ARTICHOKE HEARTS V
(ALITER SFONDYLI)

Boil artichokes hearts and fry.

Stew them in an earthen pot with oil, garum, pepper, rasin wine, to colour and bind.

ARTICHOKE HEARTS VI
(ALITER SFONDYLI)

Fill boiled artichoke hearts with oil and garum. Or fry them with oil and salt, sprinkle pepper and serve.

ARTICHOKE HEARTS VII
(ALITER SFONDYLI)

Boil artichoke hearts, remove the hard fiber, then pound the artichoke hearts with boiled spelt, eggs, garum and pepper. Make sausage shapes out of them, garnish with pine nuts and pepper. Wrap in caul and grill. Pour a little bit of wine garum and serve as crepinettes.

XXI.
CARROTS OR PARSNIPS

CARROT OR PARSNIP
(CAROTÆ SIVE PASTINACÆ)

Carrots or parsnips are fried with wine garum.

CARROT OR PARSNIP II
(ALITER CAROTÆ SIVE PASTINACÆ)

Salt, pure oil and vinegar.

CARROT OR PARSNIP III
(ALITER CAROTÆ SIVE PASTINACÆ)

Boil the carrots, cut, cook in cumin and oil, and serve. Color the cumin sauce *(with reduced wine)*.

APICIUS

BOOK IV
PANDECTES (THE ENCYCLOPEDIA)

JELLIED DISHES

FISH, VEGETABLE AND FRUIT DISHES

MINUTALS (MINCED DISHES)

GRUELS

STEWS

I.
JELLIED DISHES

MEAT JELLY
(SALACACABIA)

Pepper, mint, celery, dried pennyroyal, Chinese cinnamon *(laurus casia)*, pine nuts, honey, vinegar, garum, and egg yolks.
Place in an earthen pot fresh bread soaked in vinegar water and the liquid pressed out, add cow cheese, and cucumber.
Alternate with the nuts, finely chopped onions, chicken livers.
Cover completely with the sauce, *(cook)* and keep in a cold place.

APICIAN JELLY
(APICIANA)

Place in the mortar celery seed, dried pennyroyal, dried mint, ginger, green coriander, seedless raisins, honey, vinegar, oil and wine.
Crush together.
Place in a earthen pot 3 pieces of Picentian bread in a mould, interlined with pieces of cooked chicken, kid *(goat)* sweetbread, Vestinum cheese, pine nuts, cucumbers, and finely chopped dry onions.
Dispose those ingredients alternately, then cover with the sauce. Bury the pot in snow and serve.

MEAT JELLY II
(ALITER SALACACABIA)

Incomplete recipe. Complete from previous jelly recipes.

Hollow out an Alexandria bread soak in vinegar with water *(posca)*.

Place in a mortar pepper, mint, garlic, green coriander, salted cow's cheese, water, oil and wine. Serve.

II.
FISH, VEGETABLE AND FRUIT DISHES

DAILY DISH
(PATINA COTTIDIANA)

Make a paste of boiled brains. Season with pepper, cumin, sylphium, garum, boiled down grape must to two-thirds of the original volume *(carænum)*, milk and eggs. Cook it over a low fire or in a hot water bath *(bain-marie)*.

VERSATILE DISH
(PATINA VERSATILIS)

Crush pine nuts and toasted nuts with honey, pepper, garum, milk and eggs.
Add a little oil.

OTHER DISH
(ALITER PATINA)

Crush celtuce with pepper, garum, reduced wine *(caræno)*, water and oil.
Cook. Bind with eggs, sprinkle with pepper and serve.

OTHER DISH II
(PATINA FRICTILIS)

Take alexanders, clean, wash and cook. Then cool and drain them.
Take 4 brains, remove the strings and cook.
In a mortar place 6 scruples *(0.24oz. / 6.84g)* of pepper, pour garum and grind together.
Add the brains, grind again.
Add the alexanders and grind everything together.

Break 8 eggs in the mortar and a cyathus *(1.52 fl oz / 45mL)* of garum, a cyathus of wine, a cyathus of raisin wine.
Grind everything and mix well.
Oil the baking dish thoroughly *(put the mixture in the dish)* and cook on hot ashes.
When cooked, sprinkle with pepper and serve.

COLD ASPARAGUS DISH
(PATINA DE ASPARAGIS FRIGIDA)

Take clean asparagus, grind them in a mortar.
Pour water, grind finely and press through a colander.
Cook figpeckers after cleaning them.
Grind in a mortar 6 scruples *(0.24oz. / 6.84g)* of pepper, add garum and rub.
In an earthen pot, pour a cyathus *(1.52 fl oz / 45mL)* of wine, a cyathus of raisin wine and 3 ounces *(82.2g)* of oil and put it to boil.
Oil a dish thorougly, break 6 eggs to which you'll mix wine garum *(œnogarum)* and the asparagus mash.
Place the dish on hot ashes, pour the sauce and place the figpeckers.
Cook, sprinkle with pepper and serve.

ASPARAGUS DISH II
(ALITER PATINA DE ASPARAGIS)

Place chopped asparagus in a mortar. Grind, add wine and sieve.
Crush pepper, lovage, green coriander, savory, onion, wine, garum and oil.
Pour in a well-oiled pan and place on the fire.
If you wish, beat some eggs to thicken the dish and sprinkle with fine pepper.

DISH OF THE COUNTRY
(PATINAM EX RUSTICIS)

With wild grape, wild mustard *(sinapis)*, cucumbers or cabbage sprouts. Make in the same way as above.
If you like, arrange the dish over fish or chicken.

ELDERBERRY DISH
(PATINA DE SAMBUCO)

This dish was served cold and warm

Take elderberries, wash and cook in water. Strain the juice.
Prepare an oiled dish.
In a mortar place 6 scruples *(0.24oz. / 6.84g)* of pepper, moisten with garum and grind.
Add a cyathus *(1.52 fl oz / 45mL)* of garum, a cyathus of wine, a cyathus of raisin wine, and grind everything together.
Pour on the dish, add 4 more ounces *(109.6g)* of oil and put to boil on hot ashes.
Break 6 eggs on your preparation and whip to incorporate and thicken.
Sprinkle with pepper and serve.

ROSE DISH
(PATINA DE ROSIS)

Pick roses, strip off the petals, remove the white.
Put in a mortar and grind.
Pour 1½ cyathus of garum on the petals and strain the juice through a colander.
Take 4 brains, remove the nerves and grind them with 8 scruples *(0.32oz. / 9.12g)* of pepper.
Pour the rose juice and knead well.
Break 8 eggs on the preparation , moisten with a cyathus

(1.52 fl oz / 45mL) of wine, a cyathus of raisin wine and a little oil.

Oil thoroughly a pan, place it on hot ashes and pour the preparation.

When cooked, sprinkle with ground pepper and serve.

SQUASH DISH
(PATINA DE CUCURBITIS)

Place boiled and fried squash in a pan. Cover them with a cumin sauce, pour a little oil, heat and serve.

SMALL FISH DISH
(PATINA DE APUA)

Clean the small fish *(any young small sea fish)*, marinate in oil and place them in a Cuma pot *(shallow and large red earthen pots - Cumana)*.

Add oil, garum, wine and a bunch of rue and oregano.

When the fish is cooked, remove the herbs, pepper and serve.

SMALL FISH DISH II
(ALITER PATINA DE APUA)

Mash fried or boiled small fish *(any young small sea fish)* and fill a dish with it.

Grind in a mortar pepper and a little rue, moisten with garum un sufficient quantity and a little oil.

Mix with the fish, break some eggs and mix until you get a homogeneous mass.

Carefully place some sea-nettles above, without incorporating them to the mass.

Place on the smoke and when ready sprinkle with ground pepper and serve.

Nobody will be able to know what he is eating.

CREAMY DISH
(PATINA EX LACTE)

Soak pine nuts and dry them.
In a deep dish place successively medium mallows and beets, mature leeks, celery, boiled green vegetables and alexanders, a plucked chicken stewed in its own juice, boiled brains, Lucanian sausages, hard boiled eggs cut into halves, sliced Tarentinian sausages cooked in ashes, chicken liver, mashed hake *(Asellus)*, sea nettle, mashed oysters and fresh cheese.
Sprinkle each layer with pine nuts and whole pepper.
Pour over everything a sauce made with pepper, lovage, celery seed and silphium. Cook.
When cooked, pour milk and mix raw eggs to bind everything. Cook and garnish with fresh sea urchins, pepper and serve.

APICIAN DISH
(PATINA APICIANA)

Take cooked and chopped sow teats, fish meat, chicken meat, figpeckers or cooked thrushes breasts, whichever is best.
Mince everything, except the figpeckers and mix the meats with raw eggs and oil.
Crush pepper and lovage, moisten with garum, wine and raisin wine.
Put everything in an earthen pot to boil and bind with starch.
When done, take the pot off the fire with its juice and transfer by layers in a baking pan with whole pepper and pine nuts. On the bottom spread out a layer of thin pancake, pour layer of the meat, then alternate with pancakes and meat.
Cover with a final layer and sprinkle with pepper.

The meat will have been bound with eggs before being placed in the earthen pot.

EVERY DAY DISH
(PATINA QUOTIDIANA)

Mince carefully cooked sow's teats, cooked fish meat and cooked chicken meat.
Take a bronze *(aenus)* dish, break eggs in a pot and beat them.
In a mortar put pepper and lovage, crush, moisten with garum, wine, raisin wine, and a little bit of oil.
Empty into the pot and put to boil.
When boiled bind with the pieces of meat.
Fill the bottom of the bronze dish with a thick pancake layer, pour a layer of stew, drizzle with oil and cover with a thinner pancake layer.
Alternate these layers of dough and stew.
Cover with a pancake and make a vent hole on the surface.
Turn upside down into another dish. Sprinkle with pepper and serve.

SWEET VERSATILE DISH
(PATINA VERSATILIS VICE DULCIS)

Pine nuts, chopped and cleaned nuts. Roast them and crush with honey, pepper, garum, milk, eggs, a little bit of pure wine and oil.

SALTED FISH & CHEESE DISH
(PATELLA TYROTARICHA)

Take any kind of salted fish. Cook in oil and remove the bones.
Take pieces of cooked brains, the fish meat, minced chicken livers, boiled eggs and boiled soft cheese.

Heat all this in a dish. Grind pepper, lovage, oregano, rue *(ruta graveolens)* seeds with wine, honeyed wine *(mulsum)* and oil.

Cook everything on a slow fire. Bind the sauce with raw eggs.

Arrange the dish properly and sprinkle with small cumin seeds and serve.

DOGFISH DISH
(PATELLA SICCA)

Dogfish sausage. Unnerve *(debone and clean)* and mince finely.

Season with ground pepper, lovage, oregano, parsley, coriander, cumin, rue seeds and dried mint.

Form fish sausages out of the preparation and cook in wine, garum and oil.

Once done, arrange in a dish.

Make a sauce with pepper, lovage, savory, onion, wine, vinegar, and oil. Pour in the dish, put to heat and bind with starch.

Sprinkle with thyme and ground pepper.

ALEXANDERS DISH
(PATELLA EX OLISATRO)

Boil in saltpeter water and drain and place in a dish.

Grind pepper, lovage, coriander, savory, onion with wine, garum, vinegar and oil.

Pour on the dish and cook.

Bind with starch, sprinkle with thyme and ground pepper.

You can apply this recipe to any herb that you wish.

FRIED SMALL FISH DISH
(PATELLA DE APUA)

Clean the small fish *(any young small sea fish)*, beat eggs and mix the fish in.
Add *(in a pot)* garum, wine and oil and put to heat.
When boiling add the small fish.
Carefully turn over and let the fish get color.
Pour with a simple wine garum, pepper and serve.

MACKEREL & BRAINS DISH
(PATINA EX LACERTIS & CEREBELLIS)

Fry hard eggs, boil brains and remove the nerves, cook chicken giblets, all in proportion to the fish.
Arrange in a shallow pan with cooked salted fish in the center.
Grind pepper, lovage, sweeten with raisin wine *(passum)* or honeyed wine *(mulsum)*, put to heat.
When boiling, stir with a rue branch and bind with starch.

MULLET DISH
(PATINA MULLORUM LOCO SALSI)

Instead of salted fish, take mullet and scale them.
Place in a pan, add liquamen *(garum, wine and oil)* and cook.
When done, pour on the fish honeyed wine *(mulsum)* or raisin wine *(passum)*.
Sprinkle with pepper and serve.

FISH DISH
(PATINA PISCIUM LOCO SALSI)

Instead of salted fish, take the fish of your choice, clean them and put to fry with the desired oil quantity.
Add salted fish to the pan and cook.
When boiling hot, put honeyed wine *(mulsum)*, and stir.

FISH DISH II
(PATINA PISCIUM)

Scale, empty and trim your choice of fish.
In a pan place dried chopped ascalonian onions (shallots) or another kind of onions and lay the fish.
Add garum and oil. Put to cook and place in the center cooked salted fish.
Moisten with vinegar and sprinkle with wild savory.

LUCRATIAN DISH
(PATELLA LUCRETIANA)

Clean scallions, remove the green tops.
Chop and place in a pan with a little garum, oil and water.
Put to cook, and place raw salted fish.
When nearly done, add a spoon of honey, a little vinegar and boiled down grape must to half of the original volume *(defrutum)*.
Taste, if insipid add some garum, if too salty add some honey.
Sprinkle with wild savory and let boil.

MACKEREL DISH
(PATINA DE LACERTIS)

Scale and clean the mackerels.
Break and beat eggs, mix in the fish.
Add garum, wine and oil and put to cook.
When it is boiling add wine garum *(oenogarum)*.
Sprinkle with pepper and serve.

ZOMOTEGANITE DISH
(PATINA PISCIUM ZOMOTEGANITE)

Place raw fish in a pan. Add oil, garum, reduced wine, a bouquet of leeks and coriander.

Put to cook and crush pepper, lovage and a bouquet of oregano crushed on it's own.

Moisten with the fish broth, add raw eggs and mix before pouring on the dish.

Bind, when thickened, pepper and serve.

SOLE DISH
(PATINA SOLEARUM)

Beat the sole, prepare them (trim, skin, empty, wash) and place them in a pan.

Add oil, garum and wine. Cook.

Crush pepper, lovage and oregano, grind.

Moisten with the fish broth, bind with raw eggs and work into a uniform mass.

Pour over the sole and heat on a slow fire.

When thickened, sprinkle with pepper and serve.

FISH DISH III
(PATINA DE PISCIBUS)

1 ounce of pepper,
1 hemina *(9.23 fl oz / 273 mL)* of reduced wine,
1 hemina *(9.23 fl oz / 273 mL)* of spiced wine,
2 ounces of oil.

LITTLE FISH DISH
(PATINA DE PISCICULIS)

Have raisin wine, pepper, lovage, oregano, onion, wine, garum and oil.

Transfer in an earthen pot, when cooked add small cooked fish.

Bind with starch and serve.

FISH DISH IV
(PATINA DE PISCIBUS)

Take dentex, sea bream, and mullet. Prepare and fry lightly.
Cut the meat in pieces.
Prepare oysters.
Add to a mortar 6 scruples of pepper *(0.24oz. / 6.84g)*, moisten with garum and crush.
Add a cyathus *(1.52 fl oz / 45mL)* of garum, a cyathus of wine.
Place in pan with 3 ounces *(82.2g)* of oil and the oysters and put to boil.
When done, oil a shallow dish on which place the fish meat and the stewed oysters.
Put to boil. When cooked break 11 eggs and pour in the dish.
When thickened, sprinkle pepper and serve.

SEA BASS DISH
(PATINA DE PISCE LUPO)

Grind pepper, cumin, parsley, rue, onions, honey, garum, raisin wine and drops of oil.

SORB DISH
(PATINA DE SORBIA)

Hot or cold. Take sorbs, clean, and crush in a mortar.
Strain through a colander.
Take 4 cooked brains with the nerves removed.
Place in a mortar 8 scruples *(0.32oz. / 9.12g)* of pepper.
Moisten with stock and crush.
Add the sorbs and combine with 8 eggs.

Add 1 cyathus *(1.52 fl oz / 45mL)* of garum.
Heavily oil a clean pan and place in an embers stove.
After you've placed the preparation in the pan, make sure the pan gets enough heat from below, when done sprinkle with a little pepper and serve.

PEACH DISH
(PATINA DE PERSICIS)

Peel firm peaches, slice, boil and arrange in a dish.
Sprinkle with a little oil and season with a cumin sauce.

PEAR DISH
(PATINA DE PYRIS)

Boil pears and remove the center.
Crush them with pepper, cumin, honey, raisin wine, garum, and a little oil.
Mix with eggs and make your dish of this.
Sprinkle with pepper and serve.

SEA NETTLE DISH
(PATINA URTICARUM)

Take sea nettles, wash them, drain them in a colander, let dry on a board and chop fine.
Crush 10 scruples *(0.40oz. / 11.4g)* of pepper, moisten with garum and mix with the sea nettles.
Add 2 cyathus *(3 fl oz / 90mL)* of garum and 6 ounces *(164.4g)* of oil.
Heat in a earthen pan, when cooked take it out of the fire and allow to cool off.
Oil a clean pan, break 8 eggs, mix and pour in the dish.
Place the pan on hot embers and when done, sprinkle with pepper and serve.

QUINCES DISH
(PATINA DE CYDONIIS)

Cook quinces with leeks, honey, garum and strained oil (oleo defricato) and serve, or stew in honey.

III.
MINUTALS (MINCED DISHES)

SEA MINUTAL
(MINUTAL MARINUM)

Place fish in an earthernware pan, add garum, oil and wine.
Cook with finely chopped leek heads and coriander.
Form sausages with the minced fish adding clean shredded sea nettles.
Cook in a mix of crushed pepper, lovage and oregano moistened with with garum and with the fish sauce and pour in the pan.
When boiling, stir and bind with dough, sprinkle with pepper and serve.

TARANTO MINUTAL
(MINUTAL TARENTINUM)

Place in an earthen pot the white part of leeks finely chopped. Add oil, garum and sausage meat.
When done, make a sauce in the following manner: crush pepper, lovage and oregano, moisten with garum, add *(the above)* cooking broth, wine and raisin wine (passum) and mix.
Pour the sauce into the earthen pot and put to boil.
Bind with dough, sprinkle with pepper and serve.

APICIAN MINUTAL
(MINUTAL APICIANUM)

Oil, garum, wine, leek heads, mint, small fish, very small sausages, capon testicles *(testiculos caponum; "neutered" by*

burning the feet until the skin detaches), suckling pig sweetbreads. Cook everything together.
Crush pepper, lovage, and green coriander or seeds, moisten with broth, add a little oil and cooking broth with wine and honey.
Put to boil, when boiling, bind with dough and stir. Sprinkle with pepper and serve.

MATIUS MINUTAL
(MINUTAL MATIANUM)

Add in an earthen pot some oil and garum and put to heat.
Add chopped leeks and coriander, small sausages and diced cooked pork shoulder with rind.
Cook everything together and when halfway done add sliced Matian apples with the core removed.
While it's cooking crush pepper, cumin, green coriander or seeds, mint and silphium root, moisten with vinegar, honey, garum a little boiled down grape must to half of the original volume *(defrutum)* and cooking broth with a bit of vinegar.
Put to boil, when boiling bind with dough, sprinkle with pepper and serve.

SWEET PUMPKIN MINUTAL
(MINUTAL DULCE EX CITRIIS)

In an earthen pot pour oil and garum, heat and add finely cut leek heads and green coriander, cooked pork shoulder, and small sausages.
While cooking, crush pepper, cumin, coriander or it's seeds, green rue, and silphium root. Moisten with vinegar, boiled down grape must to half of the original volume *(defrutum)* and the cooking sauce, add vinegar in moderation and put to boil.
When cooked, place a hollowed out and peeled pumpkin,

diced and boiled in the earthen pot.
Bind with dough, sprinkle with pepper and serve.

APRICOT MINUTAL
(MINUTAL EX PRÆCOQUIS)

In an earthen pot pour oil, garum, wine, finely cut dried shallots, and a diced cooked pork shoulder.
When everything is cooked, crush pepper, cumin, dried mint and dill, moisten with honey, garum, raisin wine (passum), a little vinegar and some of the cooking sauce.
Add the apricots with the seeds removed, boil until thoroughly cooked.
Bind with dough, sprinkle with pepper and serve.

HARE LIVER & LUNGS
(MINUTAL EX JECINORIBUS & PULMONIBUS LEPORIS)

You'll find the way to make the hare minutal in the chapter of hare recipes.
In an eatherware pot add garum, wine, oil, heat and add chopped leeks and coriander, sausage meat, and diced cooked pork shoulder.
While it cooks, crush pepper, lovage and oregano, add cooking sauce and mix with wine and raisin wine.
Put to boil, when boiling, bind with dough. Sprinkle with pepper and serve.

ROSE MINUTAL
(MINUTAL EX ROSIS)

With the sauce described above, but with more raisin wine.

IV.
GRUELS

GRUEL
(PTISANAM)

Soak hulled barley for a day, wash it and place on the fire.
When boiled, add the necessary amount of oil, a small bouquet of dill, dry onion, savory and taro. Cook together.
Add crushed green coriander and salt for the juice and put to boil.
When well-boiled, remove the bouquet and transfer the barley into another pot while taking care that it doesn't stick to it.
Thin and move around in the pot over the taro stems.
Crush pepper, lovage, some dried pennyroyal, cumin and silphium. Then add vinegar, boiled down grape must to half of the original volume *(defrutum)* and garum. Mix well.
Put back into the pot and let cook the taro stems on a gentle fire.

GRUEL II
(ALITER PTISANAM)

Soak the cereal, chickpeas, lentils and peas. Crush hulled barley and boil with the legumes.
When well boiled, add oil.
Finely cut green herbs, leeks, coriander, dill, fennel, beets, mallows, and a tender cabbage core. Put in a pot.
Boil the cabbage.
Crush fennel seed in desired quantity, oregano, silphium, and lovage. When crushed, add some garum and pour over the porridge. Stir.
Finely chop some cabbage stems and sprinkle over.

V.
STEWS

VERSATILE STEW
(GUSTUM VERSATILE)

Cook small white beets, matured leeks, celery bulbs, boiled snails, chicken giblets, small birds and sausages.
Oil a pan, line it with mallow leaves and the vegetables mixed with the meat. Chop the other part of the bulbs *(bulbos inversos)*, damascus plums, snails, and small Lucanian sausages.
Moisten with garum, oil, wine and vinegar and put to boil.
When boiling, crush pepper, lovage, ginger and a little chrysanthemum coccineum *(pyrethrum)*. Moisten, mix and pour some sauce in the dish and let cook.
Break several eggs in a dish, whip with the remaining sauce in the mortar and bind your dish.
While it binds, make a wine garum as follows:
Crush pepper with lovage, moisten with garum and wine.
Mix in a small earthen pot (cacabulo) and sweeten with raisin wine or sweet wine, add a little oil and put to boil, then bind with starch.
Pour the dish in a bowl and remove the mallow leaves. Pour some wine garum over the dish, sprinkle with pepper and serve.

VEGETABLE STEW
(GUSTUM VERSATILE)

Cook bulbs *(onions, celery, etc)* with garum, oil and wine.
When cooked, add suckling pig livers, chicken livers and feet and small birds.
Cut in halves, and boil with bulbs.

When boiling, crush pepper, lovage, moisten with garum, wine and raisin wine to sweeten, then add some of the cooking sauce.

Pour the sauce on the bulbs, and when boiled, bind with starch before serving.

SQUASH STEW
(GUSTUM DE CUCURBITIS FARSILIBUS)

Carefully cut an oblong shape on the side of squashes, excavate and put in the cold *(water)*.

Crush pepper, lovage and oregano. Moisten with garum, add cooked brains and grind. Beat raw eggs and mix all together to form a mass. Add some garum and stuff in the not fully cooked squash. Close the squash with the previously cut piece and tie tightly, cook, remove from the water and roast.

Make a wine garum in the following manner: crush pepper and lovage, moisten with wine and garum, add some raisin wine *(passum)*, and a little oil.

Put to boil in a pot, then bind with starch.

Pour the wine garum on the roasted squashes, sprinkle with pepper and serve.

APRICOT STEW
(GUSTUM DE PRÆCOQUIS)

Peel young clingstone apricots, remove the seeds and keep in cold water.

Crush pepper and dried mint, moisten with garum, add honey, raisin wine *(passum)*, wine and vinegar.

Pour the sauce over the apricots, add a little oil and cook on a weak fire.

When cooked, thicken with starch, sprinkle with pepper and serve.

APICIUS

BOOK V
OSPREON (PULSES & LEGUMES)

PORRIDGES

LENTILS

PEAS

PEAS & BEANS IN THE POD

BARLEY AND SPELT GRUELS

GREEN PODS & STALKS & BAIAE BEANS

FENUGREEK

BEANS & CHICKPEAS

I.
PORRIDGES

JULIAN PORRIDGE
(PULTES JULIANÆ)

Soak hulled spelt, then put to boil.
When boiled, add oil and when it thickens, thin it down.
Pound in a mortar 2 cooked brains *(pork)* and half a pound of ground meat like when making sausages, place in an earthen pot.
Crush pepper, lovage and fennel seed, moisten with garum and a little pure wine.
Pour this sauce in the pot on top of the brains and meat.
Cook sufficiently, mix while adding the spelt little by little.
This porridge must have the consistency of barley cream soup.

COOKED WINE GARUM PORRIDGE
(PULTES CUM JURE ŒNOGARI COCTI)

Flavor with the sauce a fine wheat flour or spelt. Serve with pieces of pork prepared in cooked wine garum.

DOUGH & MILK PORRIDGE
(PULTES TRACTOGALATÆ)

Pour in a new *(clean)* earthen pot a sextarius of milk *(18.47 fl oz / 546 mL)* and some water, and put on a slow fire.
Dry three balls of dough and break them into pieces that you'll add to the milk.
To prevent burning, stir and add water .
When cooked, pour on capon testicles *("neutered" by burning the feet until the skin detaches)*.
If you wish to add honey and must with milk, add salt and a little oil.

II.
LENTILS

LENTILS & MORELS OR SMALL MUSHROOMS
(LENTICULA EX SPONGIOLIS SIVE FUNGULIS)

Take a clean earthen pot *(where you'll cook the lentils)*.
In a mortar add pepper, cumin, coriander seed, mint, rue and pennyroyal. Grind and moisten with vinegar. Add honey, garum and boiled down grape must to half of the original volume *(defrutum)*, *(mix with)* some vinegar, and pour in the pot.
Grind boiled morels and put to heat. When well boiled, bind.
Add green oil *(oleum viride, made with half-ripe olives)* in the mushroom dish.

LENTILS & CHESTNUTS
(LENTICULA DE CASTANEIS)

Take a new earthen pot and place therein carefully peeled chestnuts. Add water, salt-peter, and put to cook.
When cooked, place in a mortar pepper, cumin, coriander seed, rue, silphium root, mint, pennyroyal, and grind.
Moisten with vinegar, honey, and garum.
Add some vinegar, and pour over the cooked chestnuts.
Add oil and put to boil.
When well boiled, mix and crush in a mortar.
Taste; if something is missing add it in.
Serve in a mushroom dish and add green oil *(oleum viride, made with half-ripe olives)*.

LENTILS ANOTHER WAY
(ALITER LENTICULAM)

Cook lentils. When skimmed, top up with leek tops and green coriander. Crush coriander seed, pennyroyal, silphium root, mint seed and rue seed. Moisten with vinegar, add honey, garum, vinegar, some boiled down grape must to half of the original volume *(defrutum)*, then add oil, stir and add what may be needed. Bind with starch, add green oil *(oleum viride, made with half-ripe olives)*, sprinkle with pepper and serve.

III.
PEAS

PEAS
(PISA)

Cook peas. When skimmed, lay leeks, coriander and cumin on top.
Crush pepper, lovage, caraway, dill and green basil. Moisten with garum: wine and some garum, and put to boil. When done, stir.
If something is missing, add and serve.

PEA TIMBALE
(PISA FARSILIS)

Cook peas with oil and sow's belly and place in an earthen pot garum, leek heads, green coriander and put to cook.
Cut small dices of sausage meat, similarly cook thrushes or other small bird, or minced chicken and nearly cooked diced *(pork)* brain. Cook Lucanian sausages in the cooking sauce, boil pork shoulder, cook leeks in water and roast pine nuts.
Crush pepper, lovage, oregano and ginger. Dilute with the belly cooking sauce.
Take an angular dish suitable for turning over, oil well and line with caul.
Sprinkle a layer of pine nuts upon which put peas covering the bottom of the dish.
On top of this arrange the pork shoulder meat, leeks and sliced Lucanian sausages.
Cover with another layer of peas, on which you'll place another layer of the remaining ingredients until the dish is filled.

End with one last layer of peas, using everything. Bake in oven or on a slow fire until it thickens.
Make hard boiled eggs, remove the yolks and place the whites in a mortar with white pepper, pine nuts, honey, white wine and some garum. Grind and boil the sauce in a pan.
When boiled, turn out the peas on a dish and pour the sauce on, which is called white sauce.

INDIGO PEAS
(PISA INDICA)

Cook peas. When skimmed, finely chop leeks and coriander and place in a pot to boil.
Take small cuttlefish that you'll cook with their ink sac. Add oil, garum and wine, a bunch of leek and coriander, and cook.
When cooked, crush pepper, lovage, oregano and a little caraway. Moisten with the cooking sauce, add wine and some raisin wine.
Finely mince the fish and incorporate with the peas. Sprinkle with pepper.

PEA ANOTHER WAY
(PISA)

Cook peas, churn and place in the cold. When cooled off stop stirring.
Finely chop an onion, egg white, oil and season with salt and some vinegar. Place in a mushroom dish and sprinkle over a yolk passed through a colander, add green oil *(oleum viride, made with half-ripe olives)* and serve.

VITELLIUS PEAS
(PISA VITELLIANA SIVE FABA)

Cook peas and smoothen them.
Crush pepper, lovage, ginger, and on the condiments put hard boiled egg yolks, 3 ounces *(82.2 grams)* of honey. Mix with garum, wine and vinegar.
Place everything in an earthen pot, add oil and put to boil.
Season the peas with the sauce and smoothen. If bitter, put honey and serve.

PEAS OR FAVA BEANS
(ALITER PISA SIVE FABA)

When skimmed, grind garum, honey, boiled down grape must to two-thirds of the original volume *(carænum)*, cumin, rue celery seed, oil and wine, and mix.
Sprinkle with ground pepper and serve with sausage.

PEAS OR FAVA BEANS ANOTHER WAY
(ALITER PISA SIVE FABA)

Skim peas or beans. Season with crushed Parthian silphium, garum and boiled down grape must to two-thirds of the original volume *(carænum)*.
Pour a little oil over and serve.

ADULTEROUS PEAS
(PISA ADULTERA VERSATILIS)
Incomplete Recipe

Cook peas. In an earthen pot put brains or small birds or boneless thrushes breasts, lucanian sausages, chicken livers and giblets.
Add garum and oil, a bunch of leek heads, green coriander finely chopped and cook with the brains.
Crush pepper and lovage with garum.

VITELLIUS PEAS OR FAVA BEANS
(PISA SIVE FABA VITELLIANA)

Cook peas or beans. When skimmed, add leeks, coriander and mallow flowers. While cooking, crush pepper, lovage, oregano and fennel seed. Moisten with garum and wine in an earthen pot. Add oil, when boiling, stir.

Pour green oil *(oleum viride, made with half-ripe olives)* on top and serve.

IV.
PEAS & BEANS IN THE POD

FAVA BEANS IN THE POD
(CONCHICLA CUM FABA)

Cook. Crush pepper, lovage, cumin and green coriander.
Moisten with garum and wine, and some *(more)* garum.
Pour the sauce in an earthen pot, add oil, heat on a slow fire and serve.

APICIAN FAVA BEANS
(CONCHICLA APICIANA)

Take a clean Cumae vase, where you'll cook the peas and put sliced lucanian sausages, pork sausage meat, ground meat and pork shoulder.
Crush pepper, lovage, oregano, dill, dry onion, green coriander and moisten with garum. Add wine and some garum, put in Cumae vase.
Add oil so the dish can absorb it, cook on a slow fire to heat and serve.

SIMPLE PEAS IN THEIR POD
(CONCHICLA DE PISA SIMPLICI)

Cook the peas.
When skimmed, add a bunch of leeks and coriander.
While being cooked, crush pepper, lovage, oregano and a bunch of those crushed herbs.
Moisten with garum, wine and some garum.
Put in earthen pot, add oil and cook on a slow fire, serve.

COMMODUS PEAS IN THEIR POD
(CONCHICLA COMMODIANA)

Cook the peas.

When skimmed, crush pepper, lovage, dill, and dry onion moistened with garum. Add wine and some garum.

Place in an earthen pot, combine 4 eggs for each sextarius *(18.47 fl oz / 546 mL)* of peas.

Place in a Cumae vase and on the fire to thicken, and serve.

PEAS IN THEIR POD ANOTHER WAY
(ALITER CONCHICLAM)

Prepare a chicken, cut into small pieces.

Finely chop an onion, coriander and brains with the nerves removed.

With the chicken place garum, oil and wine and heat.

When cooked, add the chopped onion and coriander.

Take the chicken out, bone it. Cook the peas separately without seasoning them.

Pass the peas through a colander and arrange them alternately *(with the meat)*.

Crush pepper and cumin, pour in the cooking broth and mix in 2 eggs. Pour over the dish, cover with whole peas or garnish with pine nuts, cook on a slow fire and serve.

STUFFED CHICKEN OR SUCKLING PIG
(CONCHICLATUS PULLUS VEL PORCELLUS)

Bone chicken from the breast and tie the stretched out legs together.

Prepare the filling by alternating washed peas with brains, Lucanian sausages, and other similar things.

Crush pepper, lovage, oregano and ginger, moisten with garum, some raisin wine *(passum)* and wine. Make it boil and once boiled use some to season the pea filling and some over the chicken.

Wrap in caul, place in a covered dish and place in the oven to be cooked slowly, then serve.

V.
BARLEY & SPELT GRUELS

BARLEY OR SPELT GRUEL
(ALICAM VEL SUCCUM PTISANÆ)

Soak for a day hulled barley or spelt, wash and crush, place on the fire.
When boiled, add a lot of oil, a small bunch of dill, dry onion, savory and taro *(colocasium)* to be cooked together.
For the juice add green coriander crushed with salt and put to boil.
When well boiled, remove the bunch and transfer the barley to another earthen pot to avoid burning at the bottom.
Thin it out and strain into the pot, covering the taro stems.
Crush pepper, lovage, some dried penny-royal, cumin and toasted silphium. Stir well with honey, vinegar, boiled down grape must to half of the original volume *(defrutum)*, and garum.
Pour in the pot and cook with the taro on a gentle fire.

GRUEL ANOTHER WAY
(ALITER)

Soak chickpeas, lentils and peas. Crush hulled barley and boil with the legumes.
When well boiled, add oil.
Finely cut green herbs, leeks, coriander, dill, fennel, beets, mallows, and a tender cabbage core. Put in a pot.
Boil the cabbage.
Crush fennel seed in desired quantity, oregano, silphium, and lovage. When crushed, add some garum and pour over the porridge. Stir.
Finely chop some cabbage stems and sprinkle over.

VI.
GREEN PODS & STALKS & BAIAE BEANS
(FABACIÆ VIRIDES & BAIANA)

BEAN GREEN PODS & STALKS
(FABACIÆ VIRIDES)

Cook with garum, oil, green coriander, cumin, chopped leeks and serve.

BEAN GREEN PODS & STALKS ANOTHER WAY
(ALITER FABACIÆ VIRIDES)

Fry and serve with garum.

BEAN GREEN PODS & STALKS ANOTHER WAY II
(ALITER FABACIÆ VIRIDES)

Serve in *(a sauce made of)* crushed mustard, honey, nuts, rue, cumin and vinegar.

BAIAEN BEANS
(BAIANAS)

Finely cut boiled beans from Baia.

Rue, green celery, leeks, vinegar, oil, garum, a little boiled down grape must to two-thirds of the original volume *(carænum)* or raisin wine and serve.

VII.
FENUGREEK

**FENUGREEK
(FŒNUM GRÆCUM)**

With garum, oil and wine.

VII.
BEANS & CHICKPEAS

GREEN BEANS & CHICKPEAS
(PHASEOLI VIRIDES & CICER)

Served with salt, cumin, oil and a little pure wine.

BEANS OR CHICKPEAS ANOTHER WAY
(ALITER PHASEOLUS SIVE CICER)

Cook in wine garum and season with pepper.

If cooked in water, serve beans and pods in a dish with green fennel, pepper, garum and a little boiled down grape must to two-thirds of the original volume *(carænum)* instead of salt.

Or more simply, as usually done.

APICIUS

BOOK VI
AEROPETES (THE BIRD)

OSTRICH

CRANES & DUCKS

PATRIDGE, GROUSE & TURTLEDOVE

PIGEONS & FATTENED DOVES

DIFFERENT BIRDS, THRUSHES, PEAFOWL, PHEASANT, GOOSE

STRONG SMELLING BIRDS

FLAMINGOS & PARROTS

GOOSE

CHICKEN

I.
OSTRICH

BOILED OSTRICH
(IN STRUTHIONE ELIXO)

Pepper, mint, toasted cumin, celery seed, dates or caryota dates, honey, vinegar, raisin wine, garum, and a little oil. Boil in an earthen pot and thicken with starch. Place the pieces of ostrich on a dish, sprinkle with pepper. If cooking in the sauce, add spelt.

BOILED OSTRICH II
(ALITER IN STRUTHIONE ELIXO)

Pepper, lovage, thyme or savory, honey, mustard, vinegar, garum and oil.

II.
CRANES & DUCKS

CRANE OR DUCK
(GRUEM VEL ANATEM)

Wash the crane or duck, dress and place in a pot.
Add water, salt, dill and cook until half done so it's hardened.
Remove and place in an earthen pot with oil and garum, a bunch of oregano and coriander.
When almost done, add a little boiled down grape must to half of the original volume *(defrutum)* to give color.
Crush pepper, lovage, cumin, coriander, silphium root, rue, boiled down grape must to two-thirds of the original volume *(carænum)* and honey. Add the cooking broth, some vinegar, empty in the earthen pot, heat, and bind with starch.
Place in a dish *(lancem)* and pour the sauce over.

FOR A CRANE, DUCK OR CHICKEN
(IN GRUE, IN ANATE, VEL IN PULLO)

Pepper, dry onion, lovage, cumin, celery seed, plums or damascus plums with core removed, unfermented must *(mustum)*, vinegar, garum, boiled down grape must to half of the original volume *(defrutum)*, oil and cook.

COOKING CRANE
(GRUEM CUM COQUIS)

When boiling the crane, place the head out of the water. When the crane is done, wrap in a hot towel and pull the head off with the nerves so that the meat and bones remain. For it cannot be eaten with the nerves.

CRANE OR DUCK WITH TURNIPS
(GRUEM VEL ANATEM EX RAPIS)

Wash, dress and boil until half done in a pot with salt and dill.
Cook the turnips, clean, remove from the pot and clean again.
Place the duck in an earthen pot with oil, garum and a bunch of leeks and coriander. Cut finely the turnips, place on top and moderately cook. then add boiled down grape must to half of the original volume *(defrutum)* to color.
Prepare a sauce with pepper, cumin, coriander, and silphium root. Moisten with vinegar and cooking broth.
Pour on the duck, put to boil and when boiling, thicken with starch. Add the turnips on top, sprinkle with pepper and serve.

BOILED CRANE OR DUCK
(IN GRUEM VEL ANATEM ELIXAM)

Pepper, lovage, cumin, dried coriander, mint, oregano, pine nuts, caryota dates, garum, oil, honey mustard and wine.

BOILED CRANE OR DUCK II
(ALITER IN GRUE VEL ANATE ELIXA)

Pepper, lovage, celery seed, arugula or coriander, mint, caryota dates, honey, vinegar, garum, boiled down grape must to half of the original volume *(defrutum)*, and mustard.
Use the same sauce if roasting in an earthen pot.

ROASTED CRANE OR DUCK
(GRUEM VEL ANATEM ASSAM)

Pour this sauce: crush pepper, lovage, oregano, garum, honey, a little vinegar, and oil. Boil it well, bind with starch, add to the sauce slices of boiled squash or taro *(colocasium)* and bring to a boil.

If you wish cook it with pork feet and chicken livers, serve in a mushroom dish and sprinkle with fine pepper

III.
PARTRIDGE, GROUSE & TURTLEDOVE

BOILED PARTRIDGE, GROUSE & TURTLEDOVE
(IN PERDICE & ATTAGENA & IN TURTURE ELIXIS)

Pepper, lovage, celery seed, mint, myrtle berries or raisins, honey, wine, vinegar, garum and oil. Use it cold. Boil the partridge with its feathers and then remove them while wet.

If the partridge is cut into pieces, cook in its own juice until hardened, boil and season when boiled.

PARTRIDGE, GROUSE & TURTLEDOVE ANOTHER WAY
(ALITER IN PERDICE & ATTAGENA & IN TURTURE)

Pepper, lovage, mint, rue seed, garum, pure wine and oil. Heat.

IV.
PIGEONS & FATTENED DOVES

FOR ROASTS
(IN ASSIS)

Pepper, lovage, coriander, caraway, dry onion, mint, egg yolks, caryota dates, honey, vinegar, garum, oil and wine.

FOR BOILED
(IN ELIXIS)

Pepper, caraway, celery seed, wild parsley *(petroselinum)*, mortar condiments, caryota dates, honey, vinegar, wine, a little oil and mustard.

ALTERNATIVE
(ALITER)

Pepper, lovage, wild parsley, celery seed, rue, pine nuts, caryota dates, honey, vinegar, garum, mustard and a little oil.

ALTERNATIVE II
(ALITER)

Pepper, lovage, silphium, moisten with garum and wine and blend.
Pour over the pigeon or dove, sprinkle with pepper and serve.

V.
DIFFERENT BIRDS, THRUSHES, PEAFOWL, PHEASANT, GOOSE.

SAUCE FOR DIFFERENT BIRDS
(JUS IN DIVERSIS AVIBUS)

Pepper, roasted cumin, lovage, mint, seedless raisins or Damascus plums, a little honey, a little myrtle wine, vinegar, garum and oil. Heat and stir with celery and savory stalks.

ANOTHER SAUCE FOR BIRDS
(ALITER JUS IN AVIBUS)

Pepper, lovage, parsley, dried mint, anise blossoms.
Moisten with wine.
Add roasted hazelnuts or almonds, a little honey, wine, vinegar and a little garum.
Pour oil in a pot over the sauce, heat and stir with green celery and catnip *(nepeta)*.
Carve the bird and serve.

WHITE SAUCE FOR BOILED BIRD
(JUS CANDIDUM IN AVEM ELIXAM)

Pepper, lovage, cumin, celery seed, grilled hazelnuts or almonds, or shelled pine nuts, a little honey, garum, vinegar and oil.

GREEN SAUCE FOR BIRDS
(JUS VIRIDE IN AVIBUS)

Pepper, caraway, indian spikenard, cumin, bay leaves, green seasoning *(green herbs like thyme, oregano, savory)*, all kinds of dates, honey, vinegar, a little wine, garum and oil.

WHITE SAUCE FOR BOILED GOOSE
(JUS CANDIDUM IN ANSERE ELIXO)

Pepper, caraway, cumin, celery seed, thyme, onion, silphium root, roasted pine nuts, honey, vinegar, garum and oil.

VI.
STRONG SMELLING BIRDS

FOR STRONG SMELLING BIRDS OF ALL KINDS
(AD AVES HIRCOSAS OMNIS GENERIS)

Pepper, lovage, thyme, dried mint, filberts, caryota dates, honey, vinegar, wine, garum, oil, boiled down grape must to half of the original volume *(defrutum)*, and mustard.
The bird will be tastier and more nutritious, and will keep its fat if you envelop it in a dough made of flour and oil and cook it in the oven.

ALTERNATIVE FOR STRONG SMELLING BIRDS
(ALITER IN AVEM)

Stuff the bird with crushed fresh olives, sew up and boil. Then remove the cooked olives.

VII.
FLAMINGOS AND PARROTS

FLAMINGO
(PHÆNICOPTERO)

Scald the flamingo, wash and dress. Put in a earthen pot, add water, salt, dill and a little vinegar.
When half cooked, add a bunch of leeks and coriander.
When almost cooked, add boiled down grape must to half of the original volume *(defrutum)* to give it color.
In a mortar, add pepper, cumin, coriander, silphium root, mint and rue, then crush. Moisten with vinegar, add caryota dates and some of the cooking sauce.
Transfer in the earthen pot, thicken with starch, pour the sauce and serve.
Do the same for parrots.

ALTERNATIVE
(ALITER)

Roast the bird.
Crush pepper, lovage, celery seed, roasted sesame, parsley, mint, dry onion and caryota dates with honey, wine, garum, vinegar, oil and boiled down grape must to half of the original volume *(defrutum)*.

PRESERVING BIRDS
(AVES OMNES NE LIQUESCANT)

Boil with the feathers. Empty through the neck.

They will be better than by suspending them over a kettle with boiling water.

VIII.
GOOSE

BOILED GOOSE WITH COLD APICIAN SAUCE (ANSEREM ELIXUM EX JURE FRIGIDO APICIANO)

Crush pepper, lovage, coriander seed, mint, and rue. Moisten with garum, a little oil and mix.

Wipe the boiled goose with a towel, pour the sauce over it and serve.

IX.
CHICKEN

RAW SAUCE FOR BOILED CHICKEN
(IN PULLO ELIXO JUS CRUDUM)

Add in a mortar dill seed, dried mint, silphium root, moisten with vinegar, add caryota dates, garum, a little mustard, and oil. Mix with boiled down grape must to half of the original volume *(defrutum)* and place on the dill chicken.

CHICKEN ANOTHER WAY
(ALITER PULLUS)

Mix a little honey with garum. Wash a boiled chicken and dry with a towel. Make incisions and pour the sauce over so it can be absorbed.
When absorbed, roast in the sauce, sprinkle with pepper and serve.

PARTHIAN CHICKEN
(PULLUM PARTHICUM)

Empty the chicken from the belly and quarter it.
Crush pepper, lovage, a little caraway, moisten with garum and mix with wine.
Place the chicken in a Cuma pot, pour the seasoning over the chicken, add silphium and wine in which it dissolved.
Cook everything together, sprinkle with pepper and serve.

SOUR CHICKEN
(PULLUS OXYZOMUS)

One big vinegar cup *(acetabulum= 18.47 fl oz / 546 mL)* of oil, a medium vinegar cup *(acetabulum= 18.47 fl oz / 546 mL)* of garum and a small vinegar cup *(acetabulum= 18.47 fl oz / 546 mL)* of vinegar, six scruples *(0.24oz. / 6.84g)* of pepper, parsley and a bunch of leeks.

NUMIDIAN CHICKEN / GUINEA FOWL
(PULLUS NUMIDICUS)

This recipe could translate to "Guinea Fowl" or "Chicken the Numidian way".

Prepare the chicken, boil it and clean it.
Sprinkle silphium and pepper and roast.
Crush pepper, cumin, coriander seed, silphium root, rue, caryota dates, pine nuts, moisten with vinegar, honey, garym, oil and mix.
When boiling, thicken with starch then pour over the chicken.
Sprinkle with pepper and serve.

SILPHIUM CHICKEN
(PULLUS LASERATUS)

Empty the chicken by the belly, wash it, dress it and place it in a Cuma pot.
Crush pepper, lovage, silphium, wine, moisten with garum, a nd mix with a little wine and garum. Put on the chicken and when cooked sprinkle with pepper and serve.

ROASTED CHICKEN
(PULLUS PAROPTUS)

A little silphium, 6 scruples *(0.24oz. / 6.84g)* of pepper, 1 acetabulum *(18.47 fl oz / 546 mL)* of oil, 1 acetabulum *(18.47 fl oz / 546 mL)* of garum, and a little parsley.

BOILED CHICKEN IN ITS OWN BROTH
(PULLUS ELIXUS EX JURE SUO)

Crush pepper, cumin, a little thyme, fennel seed, mint, rue, silphium root.
Moisten with vinegar, add caryota dates and crush with honey, vinegar, garum and mix.
Let cool your chicken, dry it, pour the sauce and serve.

BOILED CHICKEN WITH BOILED SQUASH
(PULLUS ELIXUS CUM CUCURBITIS ELIXIS)

Prepare the sauce described above, add mustard, pour and serve.

BOILED CHICKEN WITH BOILED TARO
(PULLUS ELIXUS CUM COLOCASIIS ELIXIS)

Pour the sauce described above and serve.
Stuff the chicken with taro and Ascolana Tenera olives (olivis colymbadibus), but not too much, so that there's space and won't break when being cooked in the pot.
Place the chicken in a basket and lower it down.
When boiling, lift it up frequently so it does not break.
.

ELAGABALUS CHICKEN
(PULLUS VARIANUS)

Cook the chicken in this sauce: garum, oil wine, a bunch of leeks, coriander, satury.

When done, crush pepper, pine nuts, 2 cyathus *(3 fl oz / 90mL)* of the cooking sauce. Remove the bunches of greens, add some milk.
Pour what's in the mortar over the chicken and put to boil.
Thicken with beaten egg whites.
Place in a dish and pour the sauce over. White sauce is the way it is called.

FRONTO CHICKEN
(PULLUS FRONTONIANUS)

Sauté chicken, season it with garum mixed with oil, to which is added a bunch of dill, leeks, satury and green coriander and cook.
When cooked, take it out, place on a dish and pour over boiled down grape must to half of the original volume *(defrutum)*, sprinkle with pepper and serve.

MILK & DOUGH CHICKEN
(PULLUS TRACTOGALATUS)

This recipe may be a combination of two, the sauce at the end seems superfluous.

Cook the chicken in garum, oil, wine, to which add a bunch of coriander and onion.
When done cooking, lift it out of it's sauce.
Put in a new earthen pot milk, a little salt, honey and very little water, that is, one third.
Place on a slow fire to simmer, break pieces of dough and put them little by little, constantly stirring so it does not burn.
Put the chicken in, either whole or in pieces.
Pour in a dish and cover with the following sauce: pepper, lovage, oregano, pour honey, a little boiled down grape must to half of the original volume *(defrutum)*, and some of the

chicken cooking sauce. Put to boil and when boiling, thicken with starch and serve.

STUFFED CHICKEN
(PULLUS FARSILIS)

Empty entirely the chicken through the neck.
Crush pepper, lovage, ginger, minced meat, boiled spelt, crush well cooked brains, break eggs and mix in order to make one body.
Add some garum and a little oil, whole pepper, and an abundance of pine nuts.
With this dressing stuff a chicken or a suckling pig, leaving enough room.

STUFFED CAPON
(SIMILITER & IN CAPO FACIES)

Have a chicken and dress like above, open from the chest and remove all, then cook.

CHICKEN IN WHITE SAUCE
(PULLUS LEUCOZOMUS)

Take water and an abundance of spanish oil. Stir the sauce and turn the chicken so it absorbs the sauce.
When cooked, take the chicken out with the remaining of the sauce, sprinkle with pepper and serve.

APICIUS

BOOK VII
POLYTELES (THE SUMPTUOUS)

STERILE SOW WOMBS, RIND, TENDERLOIN, TAIL & FEET

SOW'S UDDER

FIG-FED SOW'S LIVER

TID-BITS

ROASTS

BOILED MEATS & PORK SLICES

STOMACH

KIDNEYS

HAM

LIVERS & LUNGS

HOME SWEET CAKES WITH HONEY

BULBS

FARN MUSHROOMS & CAESAR MUSHROOMS

TRUFFLES

TARO

SNAILS

EGGS

I.
STERILE SOW WOMBS, RIND, TENDERLOIN, TAIL & FEET

STERILE WOMBS
(VULVÆ STERILES)

Sterile means from virgin or spayed sows.

Season with Cyrenaican or Parthian silphium mixed with vinegar and garum.

ALTERNATIVE
(ALITER)

Pepper, celery seed, dried mint, silphium root, honey, vinegar and garum.

ALTERNATIVE II
(ALITER)

Season with pepper, garum and Parthian silphium.

ALTERNATIVE III
(ALITER)

Pepper, lovage, garum and a little aromatised wine *(condito)*.

RIND, TENDERLOIN, TAILS, FEET
(CALLUM, LUMBELLI, CODICULÆ, UNGELLÆ)

Season with pepper, garum, silphium.

GRILLED SOW'S WOMB
(VULVAM UT TOSTAM FACIAS)

Roll in bran, then place in brine *(muria)* and cook.

II.
SOW'S UDDERS

BOILED UDDER
(SUMEN ELIXAS)

Boil the udders, tie with reeds, sprinkle with salt and place in the oven or roast a little on a gridiron. Crush pepper, lovage, garum, pure wine and raisin wine. Bind with starch and pour over the udders.

STUFFED UDDER
(SUMEN PLENUM)

Crush pepper, caraway, salted sea urchins.
Sew and cook this way.
Eat with alece *(the residue of filtered garum)* and mustard.

III.
FIG-FED SOW'S LIVER

WINE GARUM FOR FIG-FED PORK LIVER
(FICATO ŒNOGARUM)

Pepper, thyme, lovage, garum, a little wine and oil.

ALTERNATIVE
(ALITER)

Incise the liver with a cane.
Marinate in garum with pepper, lovage, and 2 laurel berries.
Wrap in caul, grill on the gridiron and serve.

IV.
TID-BITS

OSTIAN SKEWERS
(OFELLÆ OSTIENSES)

Pierce pieces of meat through the skin while keeping the skin.
Crush pepper, lovage, dill, cumin, silphium, and one laurel berry. Moisten with garum and grind.
Pour in a square dish *(angularem)* with the pieces of meat.
When layed there for two or three days put on a spit crosswise and place in the oven.
When done, remove them and separate them.
Crush pepper, lovage, moisten with garum and a little raisin wine *(passum)* to sweeten.
Boil it, thicken with starch, pour on the meat and serve.

APICIAN PAUPIETTES
(OFELLÆ APICIANÆ)

Bone small pieces of meat, roll into a spherical shape, tie, and place in the oven until golden. Remove them and allow to drip.
Place on the gridiron, over a slow fire, so it does not burn.
Crush pepper, lovage, chufa, cumin, garum and some raisin wine.
Place the sauce with the rolls in an earthen pot. When cooked, remove and dry.
Serve without the sauce and sprinkled with pepper.
If too fat, remove the skin when tying.
Similar paupiettes can be made with pork belly.

WILD BOAR PAUPIETTES
(OFELLÆ APRUGNEÆ)

Cook in oil and garum and put the spices.
When cooked, before removing them from the fire, add the following spices and boil together.
Crushed pepper, spices, honey, garum and starch.
It can also be boiled without garum and oil.
Boil and dry, sprinkle pepper and serve.

PAUPIETTES ANOTHER WAY
(ALITER)

Properly fry the paupiettes until almost done.
1 cyathus *(1.52 fl oz / 45mL)* of the best garum *(mackerel garum)*, 1 cyathus of water, 1 cyathus of vinegar and 1 cyathus of oil.
Mix together, send in a earthen pan, fry and serve.

PAUPIETTES ANOTHER WAY II
(ALITER)

In a pan with plenty wine garum, sprinkle with pepper and serve.

PAUPIETTES ANOTHER WAY III
(ALITER)

Previously marinate in water with salt and cumin, then fry.

V.
ROASTS

SIMPLE OVEN ROAST
(ASSATURAM ASSAM A FURNO SIMPLICEM)

Sprinkle salt generously and serve with honey.

ROAST ANOTHER WAY
(ALITER ASSATURAS)

6 scruples of parsley *(0.24oz. / 6.84g)*, 6 scruples of silphium, 6 scruples of ginger, 5 laurel berries, 6 scruples of spices, 6 scruples of silphium root, 6 scruples of oregano, 6 scruples of chufa *(cyperi)*, a little Saussurea costus, 3 scruples of pellitory *(pyrethrum)*, 6 scruples of celery seed, 12 scruples of pepper *(0.48oz. / 13.68g)*, garum and oil as much as needed.

ROAST ANOTHER WAY II
(ALITER ASSATURAS)

Crush seeded and dried myrtle berries with cumin, pepper, honey, garum, boiled down grape must to half of the original volume *(defrutum)* and oil. Heat and bind with starch. Boil the meat, roast it with salt and pour the sauce over it. Sprinkle with pepper and serve.

ROAST ANOTHER WAY III
(ALITER ASSATURAS)

6 scruples of pepper *(0.24oz. / 6.84g)*, 6 scruples of lovage, 6 scruples of parsley, 6 scruples of celery seed, 6 scruples of dill, 6 scruples of silphium root, 6 scruples of wild nard, a little pellitory, 6 scruples of chufa, 6 scruples of caraway, 6

scruples of cumin, 6 scruples of ginger, a hemina *(9.23 fl oz / 273 mL)* of garum, and an acetabulum *(2.30 fl oz / 68 mL)* of oil.

ROAST COLLAR
(ASSATURA IN COLLARI)

Boil and place in a roasting pan with pepper, cooking spices, honey and garum. Bake in the oven until cooked.
The collar can also be boiled, if you like, bake without spices and pour the hot sauce over.

VI.
BOILED MEATS & PORK SLICES

SAUCE FOR ALL BOILED MEATS
(JUS IN ELIXAM OMNEM)

Pepper, lovage, oregano, rue, silphium, dry onion, wine, boiled down grape must to two-thirds of the original volume *(carœnum)*, honey, vinegar, a little oil.
Boil, strain through a cloth and pour the sauce on the boiled meat.

SAUCE FOR BOILED MEATS
(JUS IN ELIXAM)

Pepper, parsley, spring onion, caryota dates, garum, vinegar, a little oil. Pour this sauce hot.

SAUCE FOR BOILED MEATS II
(JUS IN ELIXAM)

Crush pepper, dried rue, fennel seed, onion, caryota dates with garum and oil.

WHITE SAUCE FOR BOILED MEATS
(JUS CANDIDUM IN ELIXAM)

Pepper, rue, onion, pine nuts, garum, wine, a little seasoned wine, a little torn soaked bread, oil.
When cooked, pour the sauce.

ANOTHER WHITE SAUCE FOR BOILED MEATS
(JUS CANDIDUM IN ELIXAM)

Pepper, caraway, lovage, thyme, oregano, spring onion, dates, honey, vinegar, garum and oil.

WHITE SAUCE FOR SLICES
(IN COPADIIS JUS ALBUM)

Pepper, cumin, lovage, rue seed, damson plums, soak in wine. Add oenomel *(honeyed wine)* and some vinegar, and stir with whip of thyme and oregano twigs.

ANOTHER WHITE SAUCE FOR SLICES
(ALITER JUS CANDIDUM IN COPADIIS)

Pepper, thyme, cumin, celery seed, fennel, rue, myrtle berries, raisins, raisin wine, a little honeyed wine *(mulsum)*, stir with a twig of satury.

SAUCE FOR SLICES
(JUS IN COPADIIS)

Pepper, lovage, caraway, mint, indian spikenard leaves, egg yolks, honey, honeyed wine *(mulsum)*, vinegar, garum and oil. Stir with a fagot of satury and leeks. Bind with starch.

WHITE SAUCE FOR SLICES II
(JUS ALBUM IN COPADIIS)

Pepper, lovage, cumin, celery seed, thyme, soaked pine nuts, soaked and peeled walnuts, honey, vinegar, garum and oil.

SAUCE FOR SLICES II
(JUS IN COPADIIS)

Pepper, celery seed, caraway, satury, safflower, spring onion, toasted almonds, caryota dates, garum, oil, a little mustard. Color with boiled down grape must to half of the original volume *(defrutum)*.

SAUCE FOR SLICES III
(JUS IN COPADIIS)

Pepper, lovage, parsley, spring onion, toasted almonds, dates, honey, vinegar, garum, boiled down grape must to half of the original volume *(defrutum)*, oil.

SAUCE FOR SLICES IV
(JUS IN COPADIIS)

Chopped hard eggs, pepper, cumin, parsley, cooked leeks, myrtle berries, somewhat more honey, vinegar, garum and oil.

RAW DILL SAUCE FOR BOILED MEAT
(IN ELIXAM ANETHATUM CRUDUM)

Pepper, dill seed, dried mint, silphium root. Pour vinegar, add caryota dates, honey, garum and a little mustard. Boiled down grape must to half of the original volume (defrutum) and a little oil, and use on pork collar.

ALECE SAUCE FOR BOILED MEAT
(JUS IN ELIXAM ALLECATUM)

Pepper, lovage, caraway, celery seed, thyme, spring onions, dates, strained alece *(filtered garum)*, honey and some wine. Sprinkle some chopped green celery on top, put oil and serve.

VII.
STOMACH

PORK STOMACH
(VENTREM PORCINUM)

Empty completely the pork's stomach, wash with vinegar and salt, then with water and stuff with the following preparation: Pounded minced pork meat, three brains with nerves removed and mixed with raw eggs, add pine nuts, and put whole pepper, and a little sauce.

Crush pepper, lovage, silphium, anise, ginger, a little rue, the best garum *(mackerel garum)* and a little oil. Fill, not too much, leaving room for expansion while cooking.

Place in a pot with boiling water, lift out and prick with a needle so it does not burst. When half done, take it out and hang it into the smoke to give color.

Boil it until done in garum, pure wine, and some oil.

Open with a knife, and serve with garum and lovage.

ROASTED PORK STOMACH
(VENTREM UT TOSTUM FACIES)

Roll in bran, place in brine *(muria)* and cook this way.

VIII.
KIDNEYS

ROASTED KIDNEYS
(LUMBULI ET RENES ASSI)

Open them into two parts, spread them and sprinkle with crushed pepper, pine nuts, finely chopped coriander and crushed fennel seed.

Close to be roasted, tie together, wrap in caul, and sauté in oil and garum.

From there roast in the oven or boil on the grill.

IX.
HAM

HAM
(PERNAM)

Cook in water with a lot of figs and 3 laurel leaves. Remove the rind, cut out little squares and fill with honey. Make dough with flour and oil and lay over the ham. When the dough is cooked, remove from the oven and serve.

HAM II
(ALITER)

Simply cook in water with figs from Caria, serve on a platter with pieces of bread, boiled down grape must to two-thirds of the original volume *(carœnum)*, or preferably aromatised wine *(condito)*.

FRESH HAM
(MUSTEI PETASONES)

Cook the fresh ham in water with 2 pounds of barley and 25 figs. When done, get rid of the skin and glaze in a fire shovel full of glowing coals, cover with honey, or better yet, place in the oven covered with honey.
When it has colored, put raisin wine *(passum)* in an earthen pan, pepper, a bunch of rue, and some pure wine.
When done, pour half of the pepper sauce over the ham, and in the other half soak in broken up must bread *(mustacei)*,

When well soaked, pour the remnant of the sauce over the ham.

BACON
(LARIDI COCTURA)

Cover with water and cook with plenty of dill. Sprinkle with a little oil and little salt.

X.
LIVERS & LUNGS

YOUNG GOAT OR LAMB LIVER
(JECINORA HÆDINA VEL AGNINA)

Mix mead *(aquam mulsam)* with eggs, and add a little milk. Slit the liver to soak and cook. Wine garum, sprinkle with pepper and serve.

LUNGS
(ALITER IN PULMONIBUS)

Soak in milk and strain. Break 2 raw eggs, add some grains of salt, a spoonful of honey, mix and fill the lungs with it. Boil and cut.

?
(CONTINUATION OF PREVIOUS RECIPE BUT SEEMS LIKE ANOTHER ONE)

Crush pepper, moisten with garum, raisin wine *(passum)*, pure wine *(merum)*. Chop the lungs/liver and pour wine garum over.

XI.
HOME SWEET CAKES WITH HONEY

HOME SWEET CAKES
(DULCIA DOMESTICA)

Stuff little palms or dates, without seed, with walnuts or pine nuts and ground pepper. Cover the entrance with salt, fry in cooked honey and serve.

ANOTHER SWEET CAKE
(ALITER DULCIA)

Remove the crust of the best African must bread *(mustacei)* and immerse in milk. When soaked, place in the oven. When a bit drier, remove and pour over honey while still hot. Stipple so that it can soak up, sprinkle with pepper and serve.

ANOTHER SWEET CAKE
(ALITER DULCIA)

Remove the crust from fine wheat bread, break in rather big bite size pieces, soak in milk, and fry in oil.
Cover with honey and serve.

ANOTHER SWEET CAKE II
(ALITER DULCIA)

In a dish put honey, pure wine *(merum)*, raisin wine *(passum)*, rue, pine nuts, walnuts, boiled spelt, add crushed toasted hazelnuts and serve.

ANOTHER SWEET CAKE III
(ALITER DULCIA)

Crush pepper, pine nuts, honey, rue and raisin wine with milk. Work well with dough, cook covered with some eggs, pour honey and serve.

ANOTHER SWEET CAKE IV
(ALITER DULCIA)

Take fine wheat flour, cook in hot water and make a very hard porridge of it.
Thereupon spread on a pan, and cut like sweets when cool.
Fry in the best oil, take them out, pour honey, sprinkle with pepper and serve.
They will be better if prepared with milk instead of water.

CUSTARD
(TYROPATINA)

Take milk and estimate the necessary amount for the dish. Mix milk with honey, like with milk desserts: put 5 eggs for 1 sextarius *(18.47 fl oz / 546 mL)*, for a hemina of milk *(9.23 fl oz / 273 mL)* incorporate 3 eggs in.
Put in an earthen dish *(Cumana)* and cook on a slow fire.
When thickened, sprinkle with pepper and serve.

SPONGE EGGS WITH MILK
(OVA SPHONGIA EX LACTE)

Incorporate 4 eggs in a hemina *(9.23 fl oz / 273 mL)* of milk and 1 ounce *(27.4g)* of oil.
In a pan add a little oil and heat. Add the preparation. When one part is done, turn over into a plate. Pour over honey, sprinkle with pepper and serve.

HONEY CHEESE
(MEL CASEUM)

Curdled milk, honey, pepper, garum or salt, oil and coriander.

XII.
BULBS

BULBS
(BULBOS)

Oil, garum, and vinegar, serve with a little cumin sprinkled over.

BULBS ANOTHER WAY
(ALITER)

Cut the bulbs, cook in water, then fry on oil.
Make a sauce: thyme, pennyroyal, pepper, oregano, honey, a little vinegar, and if you like a little garum.
Sprinkle with pepper and serve.

BULBS ANOTHER WAY II
(ALITER)

Boil bulbs, mash in a pultarium (mashed food recipient), put thyme, oregano, honey, vinegar, caryota date wine *(caryotam)*, boiled down grape must to half of the original volume *(defrutum)*, garum, a little oil.
Sprinkle with pepper and serve.

BULBS ANOTHER WAY III
(ALITER)

Fry and serve with wine garum *(oenogarum)*.

XIII.
FARN MUSHROOMS & CAESAR MUSHROOMS

FARN MUSHROOMS
(FUNGI FARNEI)

Mushrooms grown under unidentified "farn" tree. Plinus said the best mushrooms grew under oaks.

Cook farn mushrooms in hot water, dry up, put in garum and pepper, that you'll have crushed with the garum.

FOR FARN MUSHROOMS
(IN FUNGIS FARNEIS)

Pepper, boiled down grape must to two-thirds of the original volume *(carœnum)*, vinegar and oil.

ANOTHER WAY FOR FARN MUSHROOMS
(ALITER)

Farn mushrooms boiled in salt water. Serve with oil, pure wine and chopped coriander.

CAESAR MUSHROOMS
(BOLETOS FUNGOS)

boiled down grape must to two-thirds of the original volume *(carœnum)* and a bunch of green coriander. When boiled, remove the bunch and serve.

CAESAR MUSHROOMS II
(BOLETOS ALITER)

Mushroom stems in garum or sprinkled with salt, serve.

CAESAR MUSHROOMS III
(BOLETOS ALITER)

Slice mushroom stems in a pan, pour eggs, add pepper, lovage, a little honey, some garum and a little oil.

XIV.
TRUFFLES

TRUFFLES
(TUBERA)

Peel the truffles, cook in water, sprinkle with salt.
Put on a skewer and lightly roast.
Place in an earthen pot with oil, garum, boiled down grape must to two-thirds of the original volume *(carænum)*, wine, pepper and honey. When boiling, bind wih starch. Adorn the truffles and serve.

TRUFFLES II
(ALITER)

Boil the truffles, sprinkle with salt, fasten on skewers and lightly roast.
Place in an earthen pot garum, green oil *(oleum viride, made with half-ripe olives)*, boiled down grape must to two-thirds of the original volume *(carænum)*, a little wine, crushed pepper and a little honey. Heat and bind with starch.
Prick the truffles so they absorb the sauce. When properly hot, dress and serve.
If you wish, wrap the truffles in pork caul, roast and serve.

TRUFFLES III
(ALITER)

Wine garum *(oenogarum)*, pepper, lovage, coriander, rue, garum, honey, wine, a little oil. Heat and serve.

TRUFFLES IV
(ALITER)

Pepper, mint, rue, honey, oil, a little wine. Heat and serve.

TRUFFLES IV
(ALITER)

Pepper, cumin, silphium, mint, celery, rue, honey, vinegar or wine, salt or garum, and a little oil.

TRUFFLES V
(ALITER)

Boil truffles with leeks. Salt, pepper, chopped coriander and the best wine. Serve.

XV.
TARO

FOR TARO
(IN COLOCASIO)

Pepper, cumin, rue, honey, garum, a little oil.
When hot, bind with starch.

XVI.
SNAILS

MILK-FED SNAILS
(COCHLEAS LACTE PASTAS)

Take snails and sponge them. Remove the membrane so they can get out of the shell. Add them in a vessel with milk and salt for one day. The following days in milk itself. Every hour clean the dirt.
When they are so fat they can no longer get back in, fry in oil, and put wine garum.
Similarly, they can be fed on a milk porridge.

SNAILS
(COCHLEAS)

Roast in pure salt and oil. Silphium, garum, pepper, oil and pour over.

SNAILS II
(ALITER)

Roast snails. Garum, pepper, cumin, pour generously.

SNAILS III
(ALITER)

Live snails into milk and fine wheat flour. When fattened, cook.

XVII.
EGGS

FRIED EGG
(OVA FRIXA)

Wine garum *(oenogaro)*.

BOILED EGG
(OVA ELIXA)

Garum, oil, pure wine *(mero)*. Or garum, pepper and silphium.

POACHED EGGS
(OVIS APALIS)

Pepper, lovage, soaked pine nuts. Pour honey and vinegar. Mix with garum.

APICIUS

BOOK VIII
TETRAPUS (THE QUADRUPED)

WILD BOAR

DEER

ROEDEER

WILD SHEEP

BEEF OR VEAL

KID OR LAMB

SUCKLING PIG

HARE

DORMOUSE

I.
WILD BOAR

PREPARATION OF WILD BOAR
(APER ITA CONDITUR)

Sponge, sprinkle with salt and crushed cumin and leave.
The next day, place in the oven. When done, pour a sauce made of crushed pepper.
A sauce for boar: honey, garum, boiled down grape must to two-thirds of the original volume *(carænum)*, and raisin wine *(passum)*.

PREPARATION OF WILD BOAR II
(ALITER IN APRO)

Boil the boar in sea water with sprigs of laurel.
When done nice, remove the skin.
Serve with salt, mustard and vinegar.

PREPARATION OF WILD BOAR III
(ALITER IN APRO)

Crush pepper, lovage, oregano, seedless myrtle berries, coriander and onions. Pour honey, wine, garum and a little oil. Boil and bind with starch. Pour this sauce over the oven-cooked boar.
Proceed equally for any kind of game.

BOILING SAUCE FOR ROAST BOAR
(JURA FERVENTIA IN APRUM ASSUM)

Pepper, toasted cumin, celery seed, mint, thyme, satury, safflower, toasted pine nuts or toasted almonds, honey, wine, garum, vinegar, a little oil.

BOILING SAUCE FOR ROAST BOAR II
(ALITER)

Pepper, lovage, celery seed, mint, thyme, toasted pine nuts, wine. Wine, vinegar, garum and a little oil.
When the simple sauce has boiled, incorporate the crushed preparation and stir with a bunch of onion and rue.
If you want to make the sauce richer, bind with liquid egg whites, stirring gently.
Sprinkle with crushed pepper and serve.

SAUCE FOR BOILED BOAR
(JUS IN APRUM ELIXUM)

Pepper, lovage, cumin, silphium, oregano, pine nuts, caryota dates. Mustard, vinegar, garum and oil.

COLD SAUCE FOR BOILED BOAR
(JUS FRIGIDUM IN APRUM ELIXUM)

Pepper, cumin, lovage, toasted coriander seed, dill seed, celery seed, thyme, oregano, spring onion, honey, vinegar, mustard, garum and oil.

COLD SAUCE FOR BOILED BOAR II
(ALITER JUS FRIGIDUM IN APRUM ELIXUM)

Pepper, lovage, cumin, dill seed, thyme, oregano, a little silphium, rather more rocket seed.
Pour pure wine, add some green seasoning herbs, onion, toasted hazelnuts or almonds, dates, honey, vinegar, some pure wine.

Colour with boiled down grape must to half of the original volume *(defrutum)*. Garum, oil.

SAUCE FOR BOAR
(ALITER IN APRO)

Crush pepper, lovage, oregano, celery seed, silphium root, cumin, fennel seed, rue. Garum, wine and raisin wine *(passum)*. Heat, when boiling, bind with starch, cover the boar and serve.

STUFFED BOAR HAM
(PERNA APRUNA ITA IMPLETUR)

Place a stick where the joint of the ham is to separate the skin from the meat. With a funnel introduce the condiments to fill entirely.
Crush pepper, laurel berries, rue. If you wish, add silphium. The best garum *(mackerel garum)*, boiled down grape must to two-thirds of the original volume *(carænum)*, and a few drops of green oil *(oleum viride, made with half-ripe olives)*.
When done filling, tie the parts and place in a stock pot *(zema)*. Boil in sea water with sprigs of laurel and dill.

II.
DEER

SAUCE FOR DEER
(JUS IN CERVUM)

Crush pepper, lovage, caraway, oregano, celery seed, silphium root, fennel seed. Moisten with garum, wine, raisin wine *(passum)*, and a little oil.
When boiling, bind with starch, immerse the cooked venison meat and serve.

FOR BUCK
(IN PLATYCEROTE)

Similarly season a buck, or any other type of venison.

ANOTHER WAY
(ALITER)

Boil and lightly roast the deer.
Crush pepper, lovage, caraway, celery seed. Pour honey, vinegar, garum and oil. Heat, bind with starch and pour over the roast.

SAUCE FOR DEER
(JUS IN CERVO)

Pepper, lovage, onion, oregano, pine nuts, caryota dates. Honey, garum, mustard, vinegar and oil.

DEER SEASONING
(CERVINÆ CONDITURA)

Pepper, cumin, condiments, parsley, onion, rue, mint. Honey, garum, raisin wine *(passum)*, boiled down grape must to two-thirds of the original volume *(carœnum)*, and a little oil. Bind with starch when boiling.

BOILING SAUCE FOR DEER
(JURA FERVENTIA IN CERVO)

Pepper, lovage, parsley, cumin, toasted pine nuts or toasted almonds. Pour honey, vinegar, wine, a little oil, garum. Stir the sauce.

FOR ROAST DEER
(IN CERVINAM ASSAM)

Pepper, indian spikenard leaves, celery seed, dry onion, green rue. Honey, vinegar, garum. Add caryota dates, raisins and oil.

ANOTHER BOILING SAUCE FOR ROAST DEER
(ALITER IN CERVUM ASSUM JURA FERVENTIA)

Pepper, lovage, parsley, macerated Damascus plums. Wine, honey, vinegar, garum and a little oil. Stir with leeks and satury.

III.
ROE DEER

SAUCE FOR ROE DEER
(JUS IN CAPREA)

Pepper, lovage, caraway, cumin, parsley, rue seed. Honey, mustard, vinegar, garum and oil.

SAUCE FOR ROAST ROE DEER
(JUS IN CAPREA ASSA)

Pepper, herbs *(condimentum)*, rue, onion. Honey, garum, raisin wine *(passum)*, a little oil. Bind with starch when it has boiled.

ANOTHER SAUCE FOR ROE DEER
(ALITER JUS IN CAPREA)

Pepper, herbs *(condimentum)*, parsley, a little oregano, rue. Honey, garum, raisin wine *(passum)*, a little oil. Bind with starch when it has boiled.

IV.
WILD SHEEP

HOT SAUCE FOR WILD SHEEP
(JUS IN OVI FERO FERVEAS)

Pepper, lovage, cumin, dry mint, thyme, silphium. Moisten with wine. Add macerated plums. Honey, wine, garum, vinegar, raisin wine *(passum)* to colour, oil. Stir with a bunch of oregano and dry mint.

HOT SAUCE FOR ALL KIND
OF BOILED OR ROAST VENISON
(JUS IN VENATIONIBUS OMNIBUS ELIXIS ET ASSIS)

8 scruples *(0.32oz. / 9.12g)* of pepper,
6 scruples *(0.24oz. / 6.84g)* of rue, lovage, celery seed, juniper, thyme, dry mint,
3 scruples *(0.12oz / 3.42g)* of pennyroyal.
Reduce into fine powder and mix while crushing. Add in a vessel sufficient honey and use with vinegar garum *(oxygarum)*.

COLD SAUCE FOR WILD SHEEP
(JUS FRIGIDUM IN OVI FERO)

Pepper, lovage, thyme, roasted cumin, toasted pine nuts. Honey, vinegar, garum and oil. Sprinkle with pepper.

V.
BEEF OR VEAL

GRILLED VEAL
(VITELLINA FRICTA)

Pepper, lovage, celery seed, cumin, oregano, dry onion, raisins. Honey, vinegar, wine, garum, oil and boiled down grape must to half of the original volume *(defrutum)*.

VEAL OR BEEF
WITH LEEKS, SETANIAN ONIONS, OR TARO
(VITULINAM SIVE BULULAM
CUM PORRIS VEL CEPIS SITANEIS VEL COLOCASIIS)

Garum, pepper, silphium and a little oil.

FOR BOILED VEAL
(IN VITULINAM ELIXAM)

Crush pepper, lovage, caraway, celery seed.
Moisten with honey, vinegar, garum, oil.
Heat, bind with starch and pour over the meat.

FOR BOILED VEAL II
(ALITER IN VITULINA ELIXA)

Pepper, lovage, fennel seed, oregano, pine nuts, caryota dates. Honey, vinegar, garum, mustard and oil.

VI.
KID OR LAMB

KID OR LAMB STEW
(COPADIA HÆDINA SIVE AGNINA)

Pepper, garum, cook with beans.
Pour garum, pepper, silphium, cumin, bread crumbs, a little oil.

KID OR LAMB STEW II
(ALITER HÆDINAM SIVE AGNINAM EXCALDATAM)

Place in the stew pot, minced onion and coriander. Crush pepper, lovage, cumin. Garum, oil and wine. Cook. Put in a dish, bind with starch.

KID OR LAMB STEW III
(ALITER HÆDINAM SIVE AGNINAM EXCALDATAM)

Add the crushed preparation in the mortar to the raw lamb. For the kid, add the preparation when cooked.

ROAST KID OR LAMB
(IN HÆDUM SIVE AGNUM ASSUM)

The kid after being cooked in garum and oil is incised and covered with crushed pepper, silphium, garum, and a little oil. Then roast on the grill, pour the sauce, sprinkle with pepper and serve.

ROAST KID OR LAMB II
(ALITER HÆDUS SIVE AGNUS ASSUS)

Half an ounce *(13.7g)* of pepper,
6 scruples *(0.24oz. / 6.84g)* of asarabacca,
a little ginger,
6 scruples *(0.24oz. / 6.84g)* of parsley,
a little silphium,
1 hemina *(9.23 fl oz / 273 mL)* of the best garum *(mackerel garum)*,
1 acetabulum of oil *(2.30 fl oz / 68 mL)*.

SYRINGIATUS KID OR LAMB
(HÆDUS SIVE AGNUS SYRINGIATUS)

Bone through the throat, so as to make a paunch. Empty entirely the intestines by blowing through the head in order to expel the excrements by the other end. Wash carefully with water and fill with a garum mixture. Tie at the shoulders and place in the oven.

When cooked, pour a boiling milk sauce. Crushed pepper, garum, boiled down grape must to two-thirds of the original volume *(carœnum)*, a little boiled down grape must to half of the original volume *(defrutum)*. When boiling, add starch.

To be safe put the roast in a netting bag or basket, tie carefully, and boil with a little salt. When it has boiled 3 times, take out and boil in the sauce described above and pour the boiling sauce over.

SYRINGIATUS KID OR LAMB II
(ALITER HÆDUS SIVE AGNUS SYRINGIATUS)

1 sextarius *(18.47 fl oz / 546 mL)* of milk,
4 ounces *(110g)* of honey,
1 ounce *(27.4g)* of pepper,
a little salt, a little silphium.

Or,
8 crushed dates,
1 acetabulum *(2.30 fl oz / 68 mL)* of oil,
1 acetabulum *(2.30 fl oz / 68 mL)* of garum,
1 acetabulum *(2.30 fl oz / 68 mL)* of honey,
1 hemina *(9.23 fl oz / 273 mL)* of good wine,
a little starch.

RAW KID OR LAMB
(HÆDUS SIVE AGNUS CRUDUS)

This recipe might be the continuation of the previous one

Rub with oil and pepper. Sprinkle with plenty of pure salt and coriander seed.
Place in the oven. Serve roasted.

KID OR LAMB TARPEIUS STYLE
(HÆDUS SIVE AGNUS TARPEIANUS)

Before cooking, dress and sew up.
Pepper, rue, satury, onion, a little thyme and garum.
Macerate the kid in the oven in a dish with oil.
When cooked, pour on the dish: crushed satury, onion, rue, dates, garum, wine, boiled down grape must to two-thirds of the original volume *(carænum)* and oil. When well reduced, put on a plate, sprinkle with pepper and serve.

KID OR LAMB PARTHIAN STYLE
(HÆDUS SIVE AGNUS PARTHICUM)

Put in the oven. Crush pepper, rue, onion, satury, stoned Damascus plums, a little silphium, wine, garum and oil.
Hot wine on the plate, take with vinegar.

KID WITH MILK AND LAUREL
(HÆDUS LAUREATUS EX LACTE)

Clean the kid, bone, remove the intestines and stomach, wash.

Put in a mortar pepper, lovage, silphium root, 2 laurel berries, a little chrysanthemum coccineum *(pyrethrum)*, and 2 or 3 brains. Crush everything and moisten with garum and some salt.

Over the mixture strain 2 sextarius *(36.94 fl oz / 1092 mL)* of milk with 2 spoons of honey. Stuff the intestines and wrap in circle over the kid. Cover with caul or parchment paper and tighten with skewers.

Place in earthen pot or dish. Add garum, oil, wine. When half cooked, crush pepper and lovage, moisten with the kid's cooking sauce and a little boiled down grape must to half of the original volume *(defrutum)*, crush, and pour in the earthen pot.

When done, dress, bind with starch and serve.

VII.
SUCKLING PIG

DOUBLE STUFFED SUCKLING PIG
(IN PORCELLUM FARSILEM DUOBUS GENERIBUS)

Clean, empty by the throat and dress. Before searing, make an opening under the ear, and fill a beef bladder with Tarento stuffing *(see p. 55)*. Attach a bird keeper pipe to the neck of the bladder and squeeze through the ear as much stuffing as possible.
Seal with parchment paper and close.
Prepare another stuffing in this manner: crush pepper, lovage, oregano, a little silphium root. Moisten with garum. Add cooked brains, raw eggs, cooked spelt, the suckling pig's cooking sauce, small birds if you have any, pine nuts, whole pepper and mix with garum.
Stuff the pig, seal with parchment paper and close. Put in the oven, when cooked, dress, anoint and serve.

SUCKLING PIG ANOTHER WAY
(ALITER PORCELLUM)

Salt, cumin, silphium.

SUCKLING PIG WITH GARUM
(PORCELLUS LIQUAMINATUS)

Empty the pig so that no part remain inside.
Crush pepper, lovage, oregano. Moisten with garum. Add 1 brain, 2 eggs and mix.

Stuff the seared pig and close tight. Place in a basket, immerse in a boiling pot. When done, remove the seal so the sauce can spread, sprinkle with pepper, serve.

STUFFED BOILED SUCKLING PIG
(PORCELLUM ELIXUM FARSILEM)

Empty the suckling pig and sear.
Crush pepper, lovage, oregano. Moisten with garum. Cooked brains as much as needed mixed with eggs, garum and pieces of cooked sausage.
Stuff the pig which has been previously seared and rubbed with garum. Tie the pig, in a basket immerse in a boiling pot.
When cooked wipe clean, serve without pepper.

ROAST SUCKLING PIG WITH HONEY AND MILK
(PORCELLUM ASSUM TRACTOMELITUS)

Clean the piglet, empty by the throat, and dry.
Crush 1 ounce *(27.4g)* of pepper, honey and wine. Put, heat, break dry dough and mix the pieces in the earthen pot. Stir with a twig of green laurel and cook until smooth and thickened.
Fill the pig with the stuffing, tighten, wrap in parchment paper, put in the oven, dress and serve.

HOT OR COLD BOILED SUCKLING PIG
WITH RAW APICIUS SAUCE
(IN PORCELLUM LACTE PASTUM, ELIXUM, CALIDUM SIVE
FRIGIDUM JURE CRUDO APICIANO)

Add in a mortar pepper, lovage, coriander seed, mint, rue and crush. Moisten with garum. Add honey, wine and garum.
The boiled hot piglet is wiped off with a clean towel.
Cover with sauce and serve.

SUCKLING PIG VITELLIUS STYLE
(PORCELLUS VITELLIANUS)

Prepare the piglet like the wild boar. Sprinkle with salt. Roast in the oven.
Add in the mortar pepper and lovage. Moisten with garum. Miw with wine and raisin wine. Heat in an earthen pot with very little oil.
Baste the roasted piglet with the sauce so that it captures it.

SUCKLING PIG FLACCUS STYLE
(PORCELLUS FLACCIANUS)

Prepare the piglet like wild boar. Sprinkle with salt and place in the oven.
While being cooked, add in a mortar pepper, lovage, caraway, celery seed, silphium root, green rue, and crush. Moisten with garum, wine and raisin wine *(passum)*, mix. Heat in an earthen pot with a little oil, bind with starch, the piglet cooked on the bone.
Crush celery seed into a powder, sprinkle and serve.

LAUREL SUCKLING PIG
(PORCELLUS LAUREATUS)

Bone the suckling pig and prepare like the wine garum suckling pig recipe *(see following recipe)*. Sear, garnish with green laurel in the center, put to roast in the oven.
In a mortar put pepper, lovage, caraway, celery seed, silphium root, laurel berries, and crush. Moisten with garum, wine and raisin wine, and mix. Add to an earthen pot with a little oil, heat, bind, remove the laurel off the piglet, sauce lightly and serve.

WINE GARUM SUCKLING PIG
(PORCELLUS ŒNOGARATUS)

Bone the suckling pig, sear, and dress. Add to an earthen pot, oil, garum, wine, water, a tied bunch of leeks and coriander.

When half cooked color with boiled down grape must to half of the original volume *(defrutum)*.

Add in a mortar pepper, lovage, caraway, oregano, celery seed and silphium root, crush. Moisten with garum and the cooking sauce. Mix with wine and raisin wine. Pour in an earthen pot, heat, when boiling bind with starch. Pour on the pig dressed on a platter, sprinkle with pepper and serve.

SUCKLING PIG FRONTO STYLE
(PORCELLUS FRONTINIANUS)

Bone the piglet, sear, and dress. Add to earthen pot, garum, and wine, a tied bunch of leeks and dill.

When half cooked, put boiled down grape must to half of the original volume *(defrutum)*.

When cooked, clean and dry, sprinkle with pepper and serve.

SUCKLING PIG CELSINUS STYLE
(PORCELLUS CELSINIANUS)

Prepare and submerge in pepper, rue, onion, satury, it's own sauce. Inject eggs through the ears and mix in a sauce cup pepper, garum and a little wine, and consume.

ROAST SUCKLING PIG
(PORCELLUM ASSUM)

Crush pepper, rue, satury, onion, half cooked egg yolks. Garum, wine, oil, seasoned wine *(condimentum)*. Boil the seasoning. Pour over the piglet in a mushroom dish and serve.

SUCKLING PIG GARDNER'S STYLE
(PORCELLUM HORTOLANUM)

Bone the pig through the throat and place inside chicken sausage meat, finely cut thrushes, fig-peckers, sausage meat from the piglet itself, lucanian sausage meat, stoned dates, smoked bulbs, snails taken out of their shells, mallows, beets, leeks, celery, boiled cabbage sprouts, coriander, whole pepper, pine nuts. Pour over this 15 eggs. Peppered garum with 3 eggs. Stitch, sear, then roast in the oven.

Slice the back of the pig and pour over this sauce: crushed pepper, rue with garum, raisin wine, honey, a little oil, when boiled, bind with starch.

COLD SAUCE FOR BOILED SUCKLING PIG
(JUS FRIGIDUM IN PORCELLUM ELIXUM)

Crush pepper, caraway, dill, a little oregano, and pine nuts. Moisten with vinegar, garum, date wine, honey, prepared mustard. Trickle oil over. Pepper and serve.

TRAGANUS SUCKLING PIG
(PORCELLUM TRAGANUM)

Bone the piglet, and prepare like the wine garum suckling pig *(p. 142)*, then hang it to smoke. The more you'll hang, the more you'll salt. Put in a pot and boil until cooked. Serve on a dish, with fresh salt.

YOUNG SUCKLING PIG
(PORCELLO LACTANTE)

1 ounce *(27.4g)* of pepper,
1 hemina *(9.23 fl oz / 273 mL)* of wine,

1 large acetabulum of the best oil,
1 acetabulum *(2.30 fl oz / 68mL)* of garum,
1 small acetabulum of vinegar.

VIII.
HARE

SOAKED HARE
(LEPOREM MADIDUM)

Parboil a little in water, then place on a roasting pan with oil and cook in the oven. When properly done, wet with the remaining oil and the following sauce:
Crush pepper, satury, onion, rue, celery seed. Garum, silphium, wine and a little oil.
Turn around several times. Finish cooking in this sauce.

SOAKED HARE ALTERNATIVE
(ITEM ALIA AD EUM IMPENSAM)

When removed from the oven, crush pepper, dates, silphium, raisins, boiled down grape must to two-thirds of the original volume *(carænum)*, garum and oil.
Pour, and when boiled, sprinkle with pepper and serve.

STUFFED HARE
(LEPOREM FARSUM)

Whole pine nuts, almonds, chopped walnuts or beechnuts, whole pepper, hare ground meat and broken eggs. Wrap in pig's caul and put in the oven.
Make another dressing. Rue, pepper, setanian onion, satury, dates. Garum, boiled down grape must to two-thirds of the original volume *(carænum)*, or spiced wine. Boil long enough to thicken and pour. But the rabbit remains in the peppered garum with silphium.

WHITE SAUCE FOR ROASTED HARE
(JUS ALBUM IN ASSUM LEPOREM)

Pepper, lovage, cumin, celery seed, hard boiled egg yolks. Pound, mix and make a ball.
In a earthen pot, heat garum, wine, oil, a little vinegar, spring onion then put your ball of spices. Stir with a fagot of oregano or satury. If necessary, bind with starch.

HARE MINUTAL
(ALITER IN LEPOREM)

Minced dish of blood, liver and lungs.
Add in an earthen pot garum and oil. While it's cooking put finely chopped leeks and coriander.
Put the livers and lungs in the earthen pot.
When cooked, crush pepper, cumin, coriander, silphium root, mint, rue and penny royal. Moisten with vinegar. Add hare livers and blood. Pound. Add honey and cooking sauce. Mix with vinegar. Pour in earthen pot. Put finely chopped hare lungs in the pot, make it boil, when boiled, bind with starch, sprinkle with pepper and serve.

HARE IN ITS OWN BROTH
(ALITER IN LEPOREM EX SUO JURE)

Clean the hare, bone, dress, and put in an earthen pot. Add oil, garum. During cooking, add a bunch of leeks, coriander, dill.
While it's cooking, put in a mortar pepper, lovage, cumin, coriander seed, silphium root, dry onion, mint, rue, celery seed and crush. Moisten with garum. Add honey and the cooking sauce. Mix with boiled down grape must to half of the original volume *(defrutum)* and vinegar. Make it boil.

When boiled, bind with starch.
Dress, pour the sauce, sprinkle with pepper and serve.

HARE PASSENIUS STYLE
(LEPUS PASSENIANUS)

Clean, bone, dress by spreading out, and hang into smoke. When colored, cook it half done. Wash. Sprinkle with salt. Immerse in a wine garum: add in a mortar pepper, lovage and crush, moisten with garum, wine and mix with garum.
In an earthen pot add a little oil, bring to a boil, when boiled bind with starch.
Sauce the roast hare , sprinkle with pepper and serve.

HARE SAUSAGE
(LEPUS ISICIATUS)

Cook and flavour the ground meat in the same manner. Combine with macerated pine nuts. Wrap in caul and parchment paper on the edges and fasten with skewers.

STUFFED HARE II
(LEPOREM FARSILEM)

Wash the hare, dress, quarter.
In a mortar add pepper, lovage, oregano. Moisten with garum. Add cooked chicken livers, cooked brains, minced meat *(likely hare lungs and livers)*, 3 raw eggs. Mix with garum.
Wrap in caul and parchment paper on the edges and fasten with skewers. Roast slowly on a low fire. Add in a mortar pepper, lovage and grind. Moisten with garum. Mix with wine and garum. Bring to a boil, when boiled, bind with starch. Bathe the hare. Sprinkle with pepper and serve.

BOILED HARE
(ALITER LEPOREM ELIXUM)

Dress, add in a dish with oil, garum, vinegar, raisin wine *(passum)*, sliced onion, green rue, chopped thyme, serve this way.

SAUCE FOR HARE
(LEPORIS CONDITURA)

Crush pepper, rue, spring onion and the hare's liver. Garum, boiled down grape must to two-thirds of the original volume *(carænum)*, raisin wine *(passum)*, a little oil, bind with starch when boiling.

HARE SPRINKLED WITH SAUCE
(LEPOREM SUCCO SPARSUM)

Prepare like the kid Tarpeius style *(recipe p. 137)*. Before cooking dress and sew.
Pepper, rue, satury, onion, a little thyme, and mix with garum. Then put in the oven and cook.
Sprinkle the sauce all over: $^1/_2$ *(13.7g)* ounce of pepper, rue, onions, satury, 4 dates and raisins. When the sauce is colored, pour on a dish, wine, oil, garum, boiled down grape must to two-thirds of the original volume *(carænum)*, stir frequently so that it may absorb all the the flavor. Then serve with dry pepper on a plate.

Although the recipe is not clear, it is likely that the sauce is served on the side, and the pieces of meat are dipped in sauceboats (acetabulum).

SPICED HARE
(ALITER LEPOREM CONDITUM)

Cook in wine, garum, water, a little mustard, dill, a leek with it's roots. When cooked, season with pepper, satury, round onion, dates and 2 Damascus plums. Wine, garum, boiled down grape must to two-thirds of the original volume *(carœnum)*, a little oil, bind with starch. Slightly boil, season the hare, and pour on a dish.

IX.
DORMOUSE

DORMOUSE
(GLIRES)

Ground pork meat with dormouse meat from every member, crush with pepper, pine nuts, silphium and garum.
Stuff the dormouse, sew and put in an earthen dish into the oven or in an oven heated from all sides.

APICIUS

BOOK IX
THALASSA (THE SEA)

SPINY LOBSTER & CRAB

ELECTRIC RAY

CALAMARI

CUTTLEFISH

OCTOPUS

OYSTER

SHELLFISH

SEA URCHIN

MUSSELS

BONITO & YOUNG TUNA

CATFISH, YOUNG TUNA & TUNA

RED MULLET

BAIAN STEW

I.
SPINY LOBSTER & CRAB

SAUCE FOR SPINY LOBSTER AND CRAB
(JUS IN LOCUSTA & CARABO INDUTA)

Chopped scalions slightly sauteed, pepper, lovage, caraway, cumin, caryota dates. Honey, vinegar, wine, garum, oil, boiled down grape must to half of the original volume *(defrutum)*. It is best to add mustard while boiling.

GRILLED SPINY LOBSTER
(LOCUSTAS ASSAS)

Open the spiny lobster allowing to see it's profile in it's shell and pour pepper sauce, coriander sauce, and grill on the grill. When they become dry, add sauce until properly grilled and serve.

BOILED SPINY LOBSTER WITH CUMIN SAUCE
(LOCUSTA ELIXA CUM CUMINATO)

Crush pepper, lovage, parsley, dry mint, a lot of cumin. Honey, vinegar, garum. If you wish, add some leaves *(folium)* and malobathron *(likely wild cinnamon)*.

ANOTHER SPINY LOBSTER RECIPE
(ALITER LOCUSTA)

Make lobster tail sausages in this way: nard leaves, remove the roe and boil.
Then cut the meat and form sausages with garum, pepper and eggs.

BOILED SPINY LOBSTER
(LOCUSTA ELIXA)

Pepper, cumin, rue. Honey, vinegar, garum and oil.

ANOTHER SPINY LOBSTER SAUCE
(ALITER IN LOCUSTA)

Pepper, lovage, cumin, mint, rue, pine nuts. Honey, vinegar, garum and wine.

II.
ELECTRIC RAY

SAUCE FOR ELECTRIC RAY
(IN TORPEDINE)

Crush pepper, rue, dry spring onions. Honey, garum, raisin wine *(passum)*, a little wine, a few drops of good oil. When it starts to boil, bind with starch.

SAUCE FOR BOILED ELECTRIC RAY
(IN TORPEDINE ELIXA)

Pepper, lovage, parsley, mint, oregano, egg yolk, honey, garum, raisin wine *(passum)*, wine, oil.
If you wish, add mustard and vinegar.
If you serve hot, add raisins.

III.
CALAMARI

SAUCE FOR CALAMARI IN A PAN
(IN LOLIGINE IN PATINA)

Crush pepper, rue. A little honey, garum, boiled down grape must to two-thirds of the original volume *(carœnum)*, a few drops of oil.

SAUCE FOR STUFFED CALAMARI
(IN LOLIGINE FARSILI)

Pepper, lovage, coriander, celery seed, egg yolk, honey, vinegar, garum, wine, oil and bind.

IV.
CUTTLEFISH

STUFFED CUTTLEFISH
(IN SEPIA FARSILI)

Pepper, lovage, celery seed, caraway. Honey, garum, wine, condiments. Heat, open the cuttlefish and pour over.
Stuff the cuttlefish in this way: Crush pepper with boiled brains with nerves removed. Mix in raw eggs until there is enough, while pepper and sausage meat.
Sew and put into a pot of boiling water until the meat is properly cooked.

BOILED CUTTLEFISH
(SEPIAS ELIXAS)

Placed in a copper pot in cold with pepper, silphium, garum, pine nuts, eggs and season as you like.

CUTTLEFISH ANOTHER WAY
(ALITER SEPIAS)

Pepper, lovage, cumin, green coriander, dry mint, egg yolk, honey, garum, wine, vinegar and a little oil. When boiled, bind with starch.

V.
OCTOPUS

OCTOPUS
(IN POLYPO)

Pepper, garum, silphium and serve.

VI.
OYSTER

OYSTERS
(IN OSTREIS)

Pepper, lovage, egg yolk, vinegar, garum, oil and wine. If you wish, add honey.

VII.
SHELLFISH

FOR ALL KINDS OF SHELLFISH
(IN OMNE GENUS CONCHYLIORUM)

Pepper, lovage, parsley, dry mint, a little more cumin, honey and garum.

If you wish, add leaves (folium) and malobathron *(likely wild cinnamon)*.

VIII.
SEA URCHIN

SEA URCHIN
(IN ECHINO)

Add in a new earthen pot a little oil, garum, sweet wine, ground pepper and put to boil. When boiled, place the sea urchins one at a time. Mix. Boil again, when cooked, sprinkle with pepper and serve.

SEA URCHIN II
(ALITER IN ECHINO)

Pepper, a little costus, dry mint, honeyed wine *(mulsum)*, garum, indian spikenard and folium *(likely bay leaves)*.

SEA URCHIN III
(ALITER IN ECHINO)

Put the sea urchins whole in hot water, cook, remove and place on a dish. Add folium *(likely bay leaves)*, pepper, honey, garum, a little oil, and bind with eggs. Cook in an embers stove *(thermospodium)*. Sprinkle with pepper and serve.

SALTED SEA URCHIN
(IN ECHINO SALSO)

Salted sea urchin with the best garum *(mackerel garum)*, boiled down grape must to two-thirds of the original volume *(carænum)*, pepper, mix and serve.

SALTED SEA URCHIN II
(ALITER ECHINUS SALSUS)

Mix with the best garum *(mackerel garum)*, and they will appear fresh like they just came out of the water.

IX.
MUSSELS

MUSSELS
(IN MITULIS)

Garum, finely cut leeks, cumin, satury, raisin wine *(passum)*, wine, mix with water in which you'll cook the mussels.

X.
BONITO & YOUNG TUNA

STUFFED BONITO
(SARDAM FARSILEM)

Stuff the bonito in this way. Bone the bonito. Crushed pennyroyal, cumin, pepper grains, mint, walnuts, honey. Stuff and sew. Wrap in paper and place in a dish above the steam. Season with oil, boiled down grape must to two-thirds of the original volume *(carœnum)*, and alece *(filtered garum)*.

BONITO PREPARATION
(SARDA ITA FIT)

Cook the bonito, and bone. Crushed pepper, lovage, thyme, oregano, rue, caryota dates, honey. Garnish a dish with sliced eggs. Pour. A little wine, vinegar, boiled down grape must to half of the original volume *(defrutum)*, and green oil *(oleum viride, made with half-ripe olives)*.

SAUCE FOR BONITO
(JUS IN SARDA)

Pepper, oregano, mint, onion, a little vinegar, and oil.

SAUCE FOR BONITO II
(JUS IN SARDA)

Pepper, lovage, dry mint, cooked onion, cooked honey, vinegar, oil. Pour. Sprinkle with hard chopped eggs.

SAUCE FOR YOUNG TUNA
(JUS IN CORDULA)

Pepper, lovage, celery seed, mint, rue, caryota dates. Honey, vinegar, wine and oil.
Also suitable for bonito.

XI.
SEA MULLET

SAUCE FOR SALTED SEA MULLET
(JUS IN MUGILE SALSO)

Pepper, lovage, cumin, onion, mint, rue, filberts, caryota dates. Honey, vinegar, mustard and oil.

SAUCE FOR SALTED SEA MULLET II
(ALITER JUS IN MUGILE SALSO)

Pepper, oregano, rocket, mint, rue, filberts, caryota dates. Honey, oil, vinegar and mustard.

XII.
CATFISH, YOUNG TUNA & TUNA

SAUCE FOR CATFISH, YOUNG TUNA & TUNA
(IN SILURO, IN PELAMIDE ET IN THYNNO SALSIS)

Pepper, lovage, cumin, onion, mint, rue, filberts, caryota dates. Honey, vinegar, mustard and oil.

XIII.
RED MULLET

SAUCE FOR SALTED RED MULLET
(JUS IN MULLO TARICHO)

Pepper, rue, onions, dates, mustard. Mix with crushed sea urchin, oil and pour this way over fried or broiled fish.

SALTED FISH IMITATION
(SALSUM IN FALSO)

Cook the liver, crush. Put pepper, either garum or salt. Add oil, hare, lamb or chicken liver. And if you wish, place in a fish shaped mold, add on top some green oil *(oleum viride, made with half-ripe olives)*.

ANOTHER WAY TO REPLACE SALT FISH
(ALITER VICE SALSI)

The second part of this recipe is corrupted

Crush cumin, pepper, garum. A little raisin wine *(passum)* or boiled down grape must to two-thirds of the original volume *(carænum)*. Mix in many crushed nuts.
Pour into a salting mould. Sprinkle a little oil and serve.

SALTED FISH IMITATION II
(SALSUM IN FALSO)

Take as much cumin as your five fingers can hold, half of that quantity of pepper, one piece of peeled garlic, and crush. Pour garum and some drops of olive oil.
This will reinvigorate a sour stomach and promote digestion.

XIV.
BAIAN STEW

BAIAN STEW
(EMPHRACTUM BAIANUM)

In an earthen pan put minced oysters, spiny oysters, sea nettles, chopped toasted pine nuts, rue, celery, pepper, coriander, cumin, raisin wine *(passum)*, garum, boiled down grape must to two-thirds of the original volume *(carænum)*, oil.

APICIUS

BOOK X
HALIEUS (THE FISHERMAN)

DIFFERENTS KINDS OF FISH
CONGER
HORNED FISH
MULLET
YOUNG TUNA
PERCH
RED SEABREAM
MURENA
SCOMBER & MACKEREL
TUNA
DENTEX
GILT HEAD BREAM
SCORPIONFISH
EEL

I.
DIFFERENT KINDS OF FISH

HERB SAUCE FOR FRIED FISH
(JUS DIABOTANON IN PISCE FRIXO)

Prepare the fish of your choice, salt and fry. Crush pepper, cumin, coriander seed, silphium root, oregano, rue, and rub together. Pour vinegar. Add date wine, honey, boiled down grape must to half of the original volume *(defrutum)*, oil. Mix with garum. Pour in an earthen pan, put to heat, when hot pour over the fried fish, sprinkle with pepper and serve.

SAUCE FOR BOILED FISH
(JUS IN PISCE ELIXO)

Pepper, lovage, cumin, spring onion, oregano, pine nuts, caryota dates. Honey, vinegar, garum, mustard, a little oil. If you wish the sauce to be served hot, add raisins.

SAUCE FOR BOILED FISH II
(ALITER JUS IN PISCE ELIXO)

Crush pepper, lovage, green coriander, satury, onion, cooked egg yolks, raisin wine *(passum)*, vinegar, oil and garum.

SAUCE FOR BOILED FISH III
(JUS IN PISCE ELIXO)

This recipe doesn't fit the title

Prepare the fish diligently. Put in the mortar salt and coriander seed, grind well. Roll the fish in, add in a pan, cover, plaster with gypsum and cook in the oven. When cooked, remove. Sprinkle with strong vinegar and serve.

SAUCE FOR BOILED FISH IV
(ALITER JUS IN PISCE ELIXO)

When the fish is prepare, add to a flat pan coriander seed, water, green dill and the fish itself. When cooked, sprinkle with vinegar and serve.

ALEXANDRIA SAUCE FOR BROILED FISH
(JUS ALEXANDRINUM IN PISCE ASSO)

Pepper, dry onions, lovage, cumin, oregano, celery seed, stoned damascus plums, put vinegar, garum, boiled down grape must to half of the original volume *(defrutum)*, oil, and cook.

ALEXANDRIA SAUCE FOR BROILED FISH II
(ALITER JUS ALEXANDRINUM IN PISCE ASSO)

Pepper, lovage, green coriander, seeded raisins. Wine, raisin wine, garum, oil and cook.

ALEXANDRIA SAUCE FOR BROILED FISH III
(ALITER JUS ALEXANDRINUM IN PISCE ASSO)

Pepper, lovage, green coriander, onion, stoned Damascus plums. Raisin wine, garum, oil, vinegar and cook.

II.
CONGER

SAUCE FOR BROILED CONGER
(JUS IN CONGRO ASSO)

Pepper, lovage, toasted cumin, oregano, dry onion, cooked egg yolks. Wine, honeyed wine *(mulsum)*, vinegar, garum, boiled down grape must to half of the original volume *(defrutum)*, and cook.

III.
HORNED FISH

SAUCE FOR HORNED FISH
(JUS IN CORNUTAM)

This fish is unidentified, but likely similar to a swordfish

Pepper, lovage, oregano, onions, seeded raisins. Wine, honey, vinegar, garum, oil and cook.

IV.
MULLET

SAUCE FOR GRILLED MULLET
(JUS IN MULLOS ASSOS)

Pepper, lovage, rue, pine nuts. Honey, vinegar, wine, garum, a little oil. Heat, and pour over.

SAUCE FOR GRILLED MULLET II
(ALITER JUS IN MULLOS ASSOS)

Rue, mint, coriander, fennel, all of them green. Pepper, lovage. Honey, garum, a little oil.

V.
YOUNG TUNA

SAUCE FOR GRILLED YOUNG TUNA
(JUS IN PELAMIDE ASSA)

Pepper, lovage, oregano, green coriander, onion, seeded raisins. Raisin wine, vinegar, garum, boiled down grape must to half of the original volume *(defrutum)*, oil and cook.

This sauce is suitable for boiled young tuna. If desired add honey.

VI.
PERCH

SAUCE FOR PERCH
(JUS IN PERCAM)

Pepper, lovage, toasted cumin, onion, stoned Damascus plums. Wine, honeyed wine *(mulsum)*, vinegar, oil, boiled down grape must to half of the original volume *(defrutum)*, and cook.

VII.
RED SEABREAM

SAUCE FOR RED SEABREAM
(JUS IN RUBELLIONE)

Pepper, lovage, caraway, wild thyme, celery seed, dry onion. Wine, raisin wine, vinegar, garum, and oil. Bind with starch.

VIII.
MURENA

SAUCE FOR GRILLED MURENA
(JUS IN MURENA ASSA)

Pepper, lovage, satury, saffron, onion, stoned Damascus plums. Wine, honeyed wine *(mulsum)*, vinegar, garum, boiled down grape must to half of the original volume *(defrutum)*, oil and cook.

SAUCE FOR GRILLED MURENA II
(ALITER JUS IN MURENA ASSA)

Pepper, lovage, Damascus plums. Wine, honeyed wine *(mulsum)*, vinegar, garum, boiled down grape must to half of the original volume *(defrutum)*, oil and cook.

SAUCE FOR GRILLED MURENA III
(ALITER JUS IN MURENA ASSA)

Pepper, lovage, catmint *(nepeta montana)*, coriander seed, onion, pine nuts. Honey, vinegar, garum, oil and cook.

SAUCE FOR BOILED MURENA
(ALITER JUS IN MURENA ELIXA)

Pepper, lovage, dill, celery seed, sumac berries, caryota dates. Honey, vinegar, garum, oil, mustard, boiled down grape must to half of the original volume *(defrutum)*.

SAUCE FOR BOILED MURENA II
(ALITER JUS IN MURENA ELIXA)

Pepper, lovage caraway, celery seed, dry mint, pine nuts, rue. Honey, vinegar, wine, garum a little oil. Heat and bind with starch.

SAUCE FOR BOILED MURENA III
(ALITER JUS IN MURENA ELIXA)

Pepper, lovage, caraway, cumin, pine nuts, caryota dates, mustard, honey, vinegar, garum oil and boiled down grape must to half of the original volume *(defrutum)*.

SAUCE FOR BOILED FISH
(JUS IN PISCE ELIXO)

Pepper, lovage, parsley, oregano, dry onion. Honey, vinegar, garum, a little oil. When boiled, bind with starch and serve on a dish.

IX.
SCOMBER & MACKEREL

SAUCE FOR BOILED SCOMBER & MACKEREL
(JUS IN LACERTOS ELIXOS)

Pepper, lovage, cumin, green rue, onion. Honey, vinegar, garum, a little oil. When boiled, bind with starch.

SAUCE FOR GRILLED FISH
(JUS IN PISCE ASSO)

Pepper, lovage, thyme, green coriander. Honey, vinegar, garum, wine, oil, boiled down grape must to half of the original volume *(defrutum)*. Heat, stir with a whip of rue branches, and bind with starch.

X.
TUNA

SAUCE FOR TUNA
(JUS IN THYNNO)

Pepper, cumin, thyme, coriander, onion, raisins. Vinegar, honey, wine, garum, oil. Heat and bind with starch.

SAUCE FOR BOILED TUNA
(JUS IN THYNNO ELIXO)

Pepper, lovage, tuna, crushed herbs *(condimenta moretaria)*, onion, caryota dates, honey, vinegar, garum, and oil and mustard.

XI.
DENTEX

SAUCE FOR GRILLED DENTEX
(JUS IN DENTICE ASSO)

Pepper, lovage, coriander, mint, dry rue, cooked quinces. Honey, wine, garum, oil. Heat and bind with starch.

SAUCE FOR BOILED DENTEX
(JUS IN DENTICE ELIXO)

Pepper, dill, cumin, thyme, mint, green rue. Honey, vinegar, garum, wine, a little oil. Heat and bind with starch.

XII.
GILT HEAD BREAM

SAUCE FOR GILT HEAD BREAM
(JUS IN PISCE AURATA)

Pepper, lovage, caraway, oregano, rue berry, mint, myrtle berry, egg yolk. Honey, vinegar, oil, wine, garum. Heat and use it so.

SAUCE FOR GRILLED GILT HEAD BREAM
(JUS IN PISCE AURATA ASSA)

Pepper, coriander, dry mint, celery seed, onion, raisins. Honey, vinegar, wine, garum and oil.

XIII.
SCORPION FISH

SAUCE FOR SCORPIONFISH
(JUS IN SCORPIONE ELIXO)

Pepper, caraway, parsley, caryota dates. Honey, vinegar, garum, mustard, oil, boiled down grape must to half of the original volume *(defrutum)*.

WINE GARUM FOR SCORPIONFISH
(IN PISCE ŒNOGARUM)

Crush pepper, rue, honey, mix with raisin wine *(passum)*, garum, boiled down grape must to two-thirds of the original volume *(carænum)*. Heat on a very slow fire.

WINE GARUM FOR SCORPIONFISH
(IN PISCE ŒNOGARUM)

Make as above. When boiling, bind with starch

XIV.
EEL

SAUCE FOR EEL
(JUS IN ANGUILLA)

Pepper, lovage, celery seed, dill, sumac berries, caryota dates. Honey, vinegar, garum, oil, mustard and boiled down grape must to half of the original volume *(defrutum)*.

SAUCE FOR EEL II
(JUS IN ANGUILLAM)

Pepper, lovage, sumac berries, dry mint, rue berries, cooked egg yolks. Honeyed wine *(mulsum)*, vinegar, garum, oil. Cook.

HERE ENDS THE TENTH & LAST BOOK OF APICIUS

Made in the USA
Columbia, SC
28 October 2024

69cce83e-756c-474e-b6f2-7920c588fc19R01